MANAGING CONFLICT
IN ORGANIZATIONS

MANAGING CONFLICT
IN ORGANIZATIONS

M. Afzalur Rahim

PRAEGER

New York
Westport, Connecticut
London

Library of Congress Cataloging in Publication Data

Rahim, M. Afzalur.
  Managing conflict in organizations.

  Includes bibliographies and indexes.
  1. Conflict management. I. Title.
HD42.R34   1985   658.3'145   85-16758
ISBN 0-275-90027-4 (alk. paper)

Library of Congress Catalog Card Number: 85-16758
ISBN: 0-275-90027-4

First published in 1986

Praeger Publishers, One Madison Avenue, New York, NY 10010
A division of Greenwood Press, Inc.

Printed in the United States of America

The paper used in this book complies with the Permanent
Paper Standard issued by the National Information Standards
Organization (Z39.48-1984).

10 9 8 7 6 5 4 3 2

To Masuda and Sayeed

Preface

Conflict is inevitable in organizations. Whether the effect of conflict is good or bad depends on the strategies used to deal with it. Managed properly, conflict can enhance individual, group, and organizational effectiveness. Unfortunately the management practitioners have sought not so much to understand and deal with conflict functionally as to find ways of reducing it. A lot of human and other resources are wasted because some people work toward the elimination or suppression of conflict. This present state of affairs can be greatly attributed to the lack of strategies and methods available for managing different types of organizational conflict.

An important question that has yet to be answered by management researchers and practitioners is: How should a manager deal with conflict? To put it succinctly, should a manager reduce, eliminate, or even increase conflict? If the manager wants to alter the level of conflict, when and how should she or he go about doing it to increase individual, group, or organizational effectiveness? And how should a manager deal with interpersonal conflict on a day-to-day basis?

This book is an attempt to address these questions to develop a design for the management of conflict at the individual, interpersonal, group, and intergroup levels. Some of the preliminary ideas of the book were developed in collaboration with Dr. Thomas V. Bonoma of Harvard Business School and reported in a journal article Managing organizational conflict: A model for diagnosis and intervention. *Psychological Reports*, 1979 *44*, 1323–1344). My recent thoughts on managing organizational conflict have been summarized in another article, "A strategy for managing conflict in complex organizations." *Human Relations*, 1985, *38*, 81–89).

The emphasis of this book is away from the resolution to management of conflict. The former implies reduction or elimination of conflict. The thesis of this book is that the management of organizational conflict involves the diagnosis of and intervention in conflict to attain and maintain a moderate amount of conflict at various levels and to enable the organizational members to learn the various styles of behavior for effective handling of different conflict situations.

This book is designed to help the practitioners for the management of conflict in complex organizations. The trainers in conflict management will find this book to be particularly useful in understanding the concepts, constructs, and theories of organizational conflict and in designing conflict management workshops and seminars. There is greater need for training in conflict management than ever before. Indeed the book comes at a time of increasing conflict and consequent frustration and tension in the workplace. The book can be used as a good supplement to courses on Organizational and Industrial Psychology, Organizational Behavior, Organization Development, and Personnel and Industrial Relations.

I wish to express my special gratitude to Dr. Om P. Bali of Martin Marietta Corporation, for reading the first four chapters of the manuscript and providing feedback. I want to express my thanks to my undergraduate and M.B.A. students at Youngstown State University during 1976–79 who participated in the development of the two instruments for measuring the amount of conflict and the styles of handling interpersonal conflict. I want to express my appreciation to several anonymous reviewers for making comments on several parts of the book. Their opinions were useful in refining some of my thoughts on conflict and conflict management.

Acknowledgments

The author gratefully acknowledges permission to reprint or adapt the following material.

Figure 2.1: Reprinted with permission of publisher from: Rahim, A., & Bonoma, T.V. Managing organizational conflicts: A model for diagnosis and intervention. PSYCHOLOGICAL REPORTS, 1979, 44, p. 1327. Figure 3.1: Adapted with permission from: Rahim, A., & Bonoma, T.V. Managing organizational conflict: A model for diagnosis and intervention. PSYCHOLOGICAL REPORTS, 1979, 44, p. 1326. Adapted with permission. Table 3.1: Rahim, M.A. (1983). *Rahim organizational conflict inventories: Professional manual.* Palo Alto, CA: Consulting Psychologists Press, p. 21. Reprinted with permission. Figure 3.2: Rahim, A. (1983). Managing conflict in complex organizations. In D.W. Cole (ed.). *Conflict resolution technology.* Cleveland: Organization Development Institute, p. 81. Reprinted with permission. Figure 4.1: Kahn, R.L., Wolfe, D.M., Quinn, R.P., Snoak, J.D., & Rosenthal, R.A. (1964). *Organizational stress: Studies in role conflict and ambiguity.* New York: Wiley, p. 30. Reprinted with permission. Tables 4.1, 6.1, and 7.3: Rahim, M.A. (1983). *Rahim organizational conflict inventories: Professional manual.* Palo Alto, CA: Consulting Psychologists Press, p. 4. Reprinted with permission. Tables 4.2, 6.2, and 7.4: Rahim, M.A. (1983). *Rahim organizational conflict inventories: Professional manual.* Palo Alto, CA: Consulting Psychologists Press, p. 5. Reprinted with permission. Figure 4.2: J.R. Hackman and G.R. Oldham, *Work Redesign,* 1981, Reading, Mass.: Addison-Wesley, p. 90, Fig. 4.6. Reprinted with permission. Table 5.1: Rahim, M.A. (1983). *Rahim organizational conflict inventories: Professional manual.* Palo Alto, CA: Consulting Psychologists Press, p. 6. Reprinted with permission. Table 5.2: Rahim, M.A. (1983). *Rahim organizational conflict inventories: Professional manual.* Palo Alto, CA: Consulting Psychologists Press, p. 8. Reprinted with permission. Figure 6.1: Maier, N.R.F. and Versee, G.C. (1982). *Psychology in industrial organizations* (5th ed.). Boston: Houghton Mifflin, p. 119. Reprinted with permission. Table 7.1: Walton, R.E., & Dutton, J.M. (1969). The management of interdepartmental conflict: A model and review. *Administrative Science Quarterly,* 14, p. 81. Reprinted with permission. Table 7.2: DuBrin, A.J. (1972). *The practice of managerial psychology: Concepts and methods of manager and organization development.* New York: Pergamon Press, p. 214. Reprinted with permission.

Contents

List of Figures

List of Tables

1

Introduction

SOCIAL CONFLICT

Conflict is an important element of social interaction. When two or more persons or groups come in contact with one another in attaining their objectives, the relationship may become incompatible or inconsistent. The relationship among such entities may become inconsistent when two or more of the entities desire a similar resource when it is in short supply, have partially exclusive behavioral preferences regarding their joint action, or have different attitudes, values, beliefs, and skills. "A *conflict* exists whenever *incompatible* activities occur" (Deutsch, 1969, p. 7). Another definition of conflict would be, "a struggle over values or claims to status, power, and scarce resources, in which the aims of the conflicting parties are not only to gain the desired values but also to neutralize, injure, or eliminate their rivals" (Coser, 1968, p. 232).

The concept of conflict is not new and has been with us for a long period of time. It received different degrees of emphasis from social scientists during various periods of history. Over the years the phenomena relating to conflict have been studied by philosophers, sociologists, economists, political scientists, anthropologists, and psychologists (Sills, 1968, pp. 220–235). Management scholars became interested in studying conflict in organizations only in recent times.

Most of the contributions to the theory of social conflict came from philosophy and sociology. A brief review of these contributions are as follows.

Among the classical philosophers, Plato and Aristotle stressed that an absence of conflict is indispensible for the accomplishment of the just form of life in the city-state. To Plato and Aristotle, "Order marks the good life and disorder the opposite. Conflict is a threat to the success of the state and should be kept at an absolute minimum, and removed altogether if possible" (Sipka, 1969, p. 7).

The seventeenth century social contact theory of Hobbes and Locke suggested that order is essential for a proper society. Hobbes was of the opinion that an absolute monarchy is necessary to control the egotism, wickedness, passion, and hostility of human beings. Although Locke was critical of Hobbes's disposition for the political order which is empowered with absolute control, he concluded that government should control conflict.

There was a distinct shift of views on conflict during the nineteenth century. Darwin indicated that biological species survive and grow by confronting the environmental challenges. Darwin and his followers (the social Darwinists) recognized the role environmental conflict plays on the human growth and development which led to the development of the doctrine of the "survival of the fittest."

During this period conflict was the key variable in the philosophies of Marx, Engel, and Hegel, not to mention Spencer and others. Hegel's dialectic refers to the process of change through the conflict of opposing forces. It asserts that every finite concept (thesis) bears within itself its own opposite (antithesis). To overcome the opposition, one must reconcile the opposing concepts by coming to a third position (synthesis). The dialectical method thus effects a synthesis of opposites. The synthesis is turn becomes a new thesis and the dialectical process continues until a fully developed synthesis (the Absolute Idea) is reached.

The dialectics of Marx and Hegel are different. Marx saw human history as full of conflict between classes which is the mechanism of change and development. He believed that this class conflict (between haves and have nots) would ultimately lead to a classless society. This new society would be free from conflict and alienation.

Among the classical sociologists who made a significant contribution to the study of the various forms of conflict was Georg Simmel (1955). He suggested that a certain amount of conflict is as essential to the proper functioning of the groups as is stability and order. He believed that in small groups such as the marital couple, "a certain amount of discord, inner divergence and outer controversy is organically tied up with the very elements that ultimately hold the group together; it cannot be separated from the unity of the sociological structure" (Simmel, 1955, pp.17–18).

There was considerable interest among the early American sociologists in the study of conflict as important social phenomena. Most of them concurred with Park and Burgess (1924) that "only where there is conflict is behavior conscious and self-conscious; only here are the conditions for rational conduct" (p. 578).

Beginning in the late 1930s, the study of social conflict began to be neglected with the publication of Mayo's (1933) work and the formulation of Talcott Parsons' (1949) structural-functional theory, which considerably influenced social science thought following World War II. The structural-functional theory assumed society to be inherently stable, integrated, and functional, and as a result, conflict was viewed to be abnormal and dysfunctional.

During the 1950s a number of theorists, particularly Mills (1959) and Dahrendorf (1958, 1959), presented viewpoints opposing Parsons' analysis (see also Bernard, 1957; Coser, 1956). Consequently, the interest in the study of the social phenomena of conflict began to grow. The publication of *The Functions of Social Conflict* by Lewis Coser (1956), which focused on the productive potential of conflict, had much to do with this renewal of interest.

Two opposing viewpoints on the outcome of conflict were presented. A synthesis of these viewpoints regarding the usefulness of conflict is necessary. A realistic view of conflict is that it has both productive as well as destructive potentials (Assael, 1969; Deutsch, 1969).

The functional and dysfunctional outcomes of conflict are as follows (Schmidt, 1974, p. 5):

Functional Outcomes

- Better ideas are produced.
- People are forced to search for new approaches.
- Long-standing problems are dealt with.
- People are forced to clarify their ideas.
- The tension stimulates interest and creativity.
- People's capacities are tested.

Dysfunctional Outcomes

- Some people may feel defeated.
- Distance between people can be increased.
- A climate of distrust and suspicion can be developed.
- Where cooperation is needed, there may be an introspective withdrawal.
- Resistance to teamwork can develop.
- People may leave because of turmoil.

The above discussion suggests that social conflict has both positive and negative consequences. If a social system has to benefit from conflict, the negative effects of conflict must be reduced and positive effects enhanced.

ORGANIZATIONAL CONFLICT

Having recognized that conflict is an important social concept, we can then look into the special case of organizational conflict. Conflict is certainly one of the major organizational phenomena. It has been observed that, "no current investigation of how organizations operate is complete without an understanding of the significance of conflict and the techniques of its management" (Robbins, 1974, p. xiii). Pondy (1969) observed that organization theories "that do not admit conflict provide poor guidance in dealing with problems of organizational efficiency, stability, governance, and change, for conflict within and between organizations is intimately related as either symptom, cause, or effect, to each of these problems" (p. 504). Content analysis of syllabi on Organizational Behavior courses for MBA students by Rahim (1981) indicated that conflict was the fifth most frequently mentioned among sixty-five topics.

Classical View of Organizational Conflict

The classical organization theorists (Fayol, 1949; Gulick & Urwick, 1937; Taylor, 1911; Weber, 1947) did not seem to appreciate different impacts that conflict can have on organizations. They implicitly assumed that conflict was detrimental to organizational efficiency and therefore it should be minimized in organizations. They prescribed organization structures—rules and procedures, hierarchy, channel of command, etc.— so that organization members would be unlikely to engage in conflict. This approach to organization and management was based on the assumption that harmony, cooperation, and the absence of conflict were appropriate for achieving organizational effectiveness.

Taylor (1911) and his associates believed that the functioning of an organization would improve if the principles of scientific management were implemented. These principles involved the development of standards and procedures, fitting of workmen to their respective tasks, provision of means to encourage each person to the utmost utilization of his capacity, and development of organization structures to control the various phases of the business. Taylor particularly insisted that the disputes between labor and management would disappear if these principles were applied. Although scientific management led to advancement in industrial efficiency, it was not without opposition. During the later part of his life, Taylor was subjected to much criticism by labor. The opposition from organized labor was due to the belief that scientific management resulted in speed-up of the workers. The unions also objected to the scientific determination of wages without resorting to collective bargaining. Scientific management did not make any provision for the effective management of disagreements between individuals and groups in an organization.

Another classical organization theorist was Henry Fayol, a French executive. Today's organization theory is greatly indebted to Fayol (1949). In some respects his work was superior to that of Taylor. Fayol advocated that the managerial functions, such as planning, organizing, command, coordination, and control, are applicable to all sorts of organized human endeavor. In addition to this, some of his organization principles, such as unity of command, span of control, division of work, etc., are widely used today. Although Fayol's approaches to management were more systematic and broader than those of Taylor, both of them as well as other classicists such as Gulick and Urwick (1937) and Mooney and Reiley (1939), saw organizations from a closed-system perspective. They implicitly assumed that conflict was detrimental to organizational effectiveness. They prescribed mechanistic organizational structures with clear lines of authority, hierarchical structures, division of labor, etc., which would encourage harmony and cooperation and suppress or eliminate conflict among members.

Max Weber (1947), a German sociologist, considered his bureaucracy to be the best form of organization, with its emphasis on rules and work procedures, rights and duties of position incumbents, division of labor, hierarchical structure of authority, impersonality, and technical competence of organizational members. Weber left no room for conflict or deviance in his model of bureaucracy. Although he was aware of some of the dysfunctions of bureaucracy he maintained that bureaucratic structures were appropriate for organizational effectiveness (Weber, 1947).

Among the classical organization theorists, Mary Parker Follet (1940) was a significant exception. Her strong behavioral orientation to management and organization in the 1920s placed her several decades ahead of her time. She noted the value of constructive conflict in an organization: "We can often measure our progress by watching the nature of our conflicts. Social progress is in this respect like individual progress; we become spiritually more and more developed as our conflicts rise to higher levels" (Follet, 1940, p. 35). She strongly advocated the need for integrative (problem-solving) method to deal with conflict.

Neoclassical View of Organizational Conflict

The studies of Elton Mayo (1933) during the 1920s and 1930s, which led to human relations movement, also emphasized the need for minimization or elimination of conflict for increasing organizational effectiveness. "Conflict to Mayo was neither inevitable nor economic. It was a result of the maladjustment of a few men on the labor side of the picture. Even after Hawthorne forced Mayo to grow, he remained firm in his conviction that conflict was an evil, a symptom of the lack of social skills. Cooperation, for him, was symptomatic of health . . . " (Baritz, 1960, p. 203). Whyte's (1951) studies, to a lesser extent, fall in this category. Both Taylor and Mayo intended to reduce conflict for enhancing the organizational efficiency, but they followed different routes. Whereas Taylor attempted to reduce conflict by altering the technical system of the organization, Mayo attempted to accomplish this by altering its social system.

Thus, it can be observed that the classical organization theorists, with the exception of Follet, did not incorporate a conflict variable into their models. These theorists "viewed conflict as undesirable, detrimental to the organization. Ideally it should not exist. The prescription was simple. Eliminate it" (Litterer, 1966, p. 178). The classicists did not, however, explicitly state that conflict should be eliminated from organizations. They, of course, implicitly assumed that conflict was not desirable for an organization and should be minimized. This approach to organization and management dominated the literature during the first half of this century.

Modern View of Organizational Conflict

Litterer (1966) argued that the above view of classical organization theorists is similar to the "view of others on the handling of tension within people. A fundamental position of many who analyzed individual behavior was that individuals were motivated by a desire for tension reduction. The prescription in both therapy and organization design therefore was to take steps or make arrangements which would reduce tension within individuals. More recently it has become accepted that *tension is normal, even desirable with the thought growing that 'healthy' personalities actually seek to increase tension"* (pp. 178–179; emphasis added).

The above line of reasoning is important in understanding the shift in conceptualization of conflict in organizations. Taking the lead from Litterer it can be observed that "healthy" organizations seek to increase intraorganizational conflict. It does not necessarily signify any organizational weakness as implied by the classical organization theorists or human relationists.

Robbins (1974) presented three philosophies of organizational conflict. The philosophy of conflict of the classicists or traditionalists, discussed earlier in this chapter, was based on the assumption that conflict was detrimental to an organization and, as such, must be reduced or eliminated. This stage was followed by the behavioralists' philosophy, which can best be described as the recognition that conflict is inevitable in organizations. They accept the presence of conflict and even occasionally advocate the enhancement of conflict for increasing organizational effectiveness. But they have not actively created conditions which generate conflict in organizations. The philosophy of conflict of the interactionists is the third philosophy, which differs significantly from the previous two. It is characterized by the following:

1. recognition of the absolute necessity of conflict;
2. explicit encouragemment of opposition;
3. defining conflict management to include stimulation as well as resolution methods; and
4. considering the management of conflict as a major responsibility of all administrators (Robbins, 1974, pp. 13–14).

Miles (1980) has summarized the significance and functions of organizational conflict quite forcefully:

> Although some theorists have regarded excess organizational conflict as the antithesis of "organization," others have begun to stress the function of conflict as a vital seed from which organizational processs, such as activation and motivation, feedback and control, power balance and coalition formation, growth and innovation, and even the institutions for channeling and resolving disputes, germinate. These functions and dysfunctions reveal both the centrality of conflict in organizational life and the complexity associated with its management. Both these features make it absolutely essential that managers and organizational designers understand the context in which organizational conflict occurs and the variety of techniques available for use in its management. (p. 129)

Organizational conflict as it stands now is considered as legitimate, inevitable, and even a positive indicator of effective organizational management. It is now recognized that conflict within certain limits is essential to productivity. However, conflict can be functional to the extent to which it results in the creative solution to problems or the effective attainment of subsystem or organizational objectives which otherwise would not have been possible. Little or no conflict in organizations may lead to stagnation, poor decisions, and ineffectiveness. On the other hand, organizational conflict left uncontrolled may have dysfunctional outcomes. Therefore, the central theme is that "too little manifestation of conflict is stagnancy, but uncontrolled conflict threatens chaos" (Hampton, Summer, & Webber, 1973, p. 670). The above discussion leads to the conclusion that too little or too much of conflict are both dysfunctional for an organization's effectiveness. A moderate amount of conflict, handled in a constructive manner, is essential for attaining and maintaining an optimum level of organizational effectiveness (Rahim & Bonoma, 1979).

Although the present attitude toward conflict is that it is essential for attaining and maintaining an optimum level of organizational effectiveness, some writers have overemphasized the dysfunctional consequences of conflict or failed to comprehend fully the functional aspects of conflict (e. g., McDonald, 1972). McDonald not only overemphasized the dysfunctional aspects of conflict at top management but his prescription included comprehensive criteria for executive selection to reduce the likelihood of such conflict (p. 59). This strategy may be able to reduce conflict, but it may also reduce the effectiveness or creativity of the top management group.

Vickers (1968) has noted the importance of enhancing the skill for resolving and containing social conflict. A study sponsored by the American Management Association shows that middle and top managers "have a lively and growing interest in learning more about both the prevention and management of conflict" (Thomas & Schmidt, 1976, p. 318). Some of the findings of this study are

1. The chief executive officers, vice-presidents, and middle managers spend about 18 percent, 21 percent, and 26 percent of their time, respectively, in dealing with conflict.
2. The respondents felt that their ability to manage conflict has become more important over the past ten years.
3. They rated conflict management as equal to or slightly higher in importance than the topics taught in AMA programs (which include planning, communication, motivation, and decision making).

SUMMARY

The study of social conflict has received different emphases at different periods of history from scholars in philosophy, sociology, economics, political science, anthropology, and psychology. Most of the contributions to the study of social conflict came from philosophers and sociologists. It is generally agreed that social conflict has both functional and dysfunctional consequences.

The study of organization theory is not complete without an understanding of the phenomena of conflict. The classical organization theorists implicitly assumed that conflict was detrimental to organizations and as a result, they attempted to eliminate it by designing mechanistic or bureaucratic organization structures. The neoclassical or human relation theorists also considered conflict to be bad, but they tried to eliminate it by improving the social system of the organization.

The modern view of conflict, however, is that it is not necessarily dysfunctional for organizations. A moderate amount of conflict, handled in a constructive fashion, is necessary for attaining an optimum level of organizational effectiveness. Recent studies show that conflict management skills are important for managers and that managers are interested in learning more about organizational conflict and its management.

Chapter 2 discusses the nature of conflict with particular emphasis on organizational conflict. Chapter 3 discusses the overall design or strategy for the management of organizational conflict. Chapters 4 through 7 provide the details for the management of intrapersonal, interpersonal, intragroup, and intergroup conflicts, respectively. The final chapter summarizes the discussions of the previous seven chapters and presents some concluding remarks. Appendixes A and B present cases and exercises, respectively.

REFERENCES

Assael, H. (1969). Constructive role of interoganizational conflict. *Administrative Science Quarterly, 14,* 573–582.

Baritz, L. (1960). *The servants of power: A history of the use of social science in American industry.* Middletown, CT: Wesleyan University Press.

Bernard, J. (1957). The sociological study of conflict. In International Sociological Association (Ed.), *The nature of conflict: Studies on the sociological aspects of international tensions*: UNESCO, Tensions and Technology Series (pp. 33–117). Paris: UNESCO.

Coser, L. A. (1956). *The functions of social conflict.* Glencoe, IL.: Free Press.

Coser, L. A. (1968). Conflict: III. Social aspects. In D. L. Sills (Ed.), *International encyclopedia of the social sciences* (Vol. 3, pp. 232-236). New York: Crowell Collier and Macmillan.

Dahrendorf, R. (1958). Out of utopia: Toward a reorientation of sociological analysis. *American Journal of Sociology, 64,* 115–127.

Dahrendorf, R. (1959). *Class and class conflict in industrial society* (Author, Trans. from German, rev. and expanded) Stanford CA.: Stanford University Press.

Deutsch, M. (1969). Conflicts: Productive and destructive. *Journal of Social Issues, 25*(1), 7–41.

Fayol, H. (1949). *General and industrial management*. (C. Storrs, Trans. from French) London: Pitman. (Originally published, 1916).

Follet, M. P. (1940). Constructive conflict. In H. C. Metcalf & L. Urwick (Eds.), *Dynamic administration: The collected papers of Mary Parker Follet*. New York: Harper.

Gulick, L. H. & Urwick, L. (Eds.). (1937). *Papers on the science of administration*. New York: Institute of Public Administration, Columbia University.

Hampton, D. R., Summer, C. E., & Webber, R. A. (1973). *Organizational behavior and the practice of management* (2nd ed.). Glenview, IL.: Scott, Foresman.

Litterer, J. A. (1966). Conflict in organization: A re-examination. *Academy of Management Journal, 9,* 178–186.

Mayo, E. (1933). *The human problems of an industrial civilization*. New York: Macmillan.

McDonald, A. (1972). Conflict at the summit: A deadly game. *Harvard Business Review, 50* (2), 59–68.

Miles, R. H. (1980). *Macro organizational behavior*. Santa Monica, CA.: Goodyear.

Mills, C. R. (1959). *The sociological imagination*. New York: Oxford University Press.

Mooney, J. D., & Reiley, A. C. (1939). *The principles of organization*. New York: Harper.

Park, R. E., & Burgess, E. (1969). *Introduction to the science of sociology* (3rd ed.). Chicago: University of Chicago Press. (Original work published 1921.)

Parsons, T. (1949). *Essays in sociological theory: Pure and applied*. Glencoe, IL.: Free Press.

Pondy, L. R. (1969). Varieties of organizational conflict. *Administrative Science Quarterly, 14*, 499–505.

Rahim, A. (1981). Organizational behavior courses for graduate students in business administration: Views from the tower and battlefield. *Psychological Reports, 49*, 583–592.

Rahim, A., & Bonoma, T. V. (1979). Managing organizational conflict: A model for diagnosis and intervention. *Psychological Reports, 44*, 1323–1344.

Robbins, S. P. (1974). *Managing organizational conflict: A nontraditional approach*. Englewood Cliffs, N.J.: Prentice-Hall.

Schmidt, S. M. (1974). Conflict: A powerful process of (good or bad) change. *Management Review, 63* (12), 4–10.

Sills, D. L. (Ed.). (1968). *International encyclopedia of the social sciences* (vol. 3). New York: Crowell Collier and Macmillan.

Simmel, G. (1955). *Conflict: The web of group affiliations* (R. Bendix & K. H. Wolff. trans.) Glencoe, Ill.: Free Press. (Originally published in German in 1908).

Sipka, T. A. (1969). *Social conflict and re-construction*. Unpublished doctoral dissertation, Boston College, Boston.

Taylor, F. W. (1911). *The principles of scientific management.*. New York: Harper.

Thomas, K. W., & Schmidt, W. H. (1976). A survey of managerial interests with respect to conflict. *Academy of Management Journal, 19,* 315–318.

Vickers, G. (1968). The management of conflict. *Futures, 4,* 126–141.

Weber, M. (1947). *The theory of social and economic organization.* (A. M. Henderson & T. Persons, Trans. from German). New York: Oxford University Press. (Originally published 1929)

Whyte, W. F. (1951). *Pattern for industrial peace.* New York: Harper.

2

Nature of Conflict

DEFINING CONFLICT

The concept of conflict was introduced in the previous chapter. This chapter further pursues the literature on conflict, especially organizational conflict, for a more theoretical understanding of its nature and implications.

The term "conflict" has no single clear meaning. Much of the confusion has been created by scholars in different disciplines who are interested in studying conflict. Systematic reviews of the conflict literature by Fink (1968), Tedeschi, Schlenker, and Bonoma (1973), and Thomas (1976) show a conceptual sympathy for, but little consensual endorsement of, any generally accepted definition of conflict. Fink (1968), in his classic review, has illustrated tremendous variance in conflict definitions. He discovered a range of definitions for specific interests and a variety of general definitions which attempt to be all inclusive.

In the organizational area, March and Simon (1958) consider conflict as a breakdown in the standard mechanisms of decision making, so that an individual or group experiences difficulty in selecting an alternative. This is a narrow conceptualization of conflict and is not very useful for research purposes. On the broad side, Pondy (1967) has argued that organizational conflict can best be understood as a dynamic process underlying organizational behavior. This is a very broad definition which excludes very little of anything transpiring in a group or individual. Tedeschi et al. (1973) take a middle position, defining conflict as "an interactive state in which the behaviors or goals of one actor are to some degree incompatible with the behaviors or goals of some other actor or actors" (p. 232). It is understood from their exposition that "actor" refers to any social entity from the dyad to the corporate body itself. Smith (1966) also take a similar position and defines conflict as "a situation in which the conditions, practices, or goals for the different participants are inherently incompatible" (p. 511). Another definition of conflict is "a *type of behavior which occurs* when two or more parties are in opposition or in battle *as a result* of a perceived relative deprivation from the activities of or interacting with another person or group" (Litterer, 1966, p. 180). The difference between the last two authors in defining conflict is that whereas Smith considers conflict as a situation, Litterer considers it as a type of behavior. However, both of these authors and Tedeschi et al. consider conflict to result from incompatibility or opposition in goals, activities, or interaction among the social entities. Schmidt and Kochan (1972) define conflict as an act of blocking. They argue that "goal incompatibility, perceived opportunity for interference, and interdependent activities among organizational subunits increase the potential for conflict" (p. 259).

Conflict is defined as an "interactive state" manifested in incompatibility, disagreement, or difference within or between social entities, i.e., individual, group, organization, etc. Calling conflict an interactive state does not preclude the possibilities of intraindividual conflict, for it is known that a person often interacts with oneself. Obviously, one also interacts with others. Conflict occurs when a social entity (1) is required to engage in an activity which is incongruent with his or her needs or interests, (2) holds behavioral preferences, the satisfaction of which is incompatible with another person's implementation of his or her preferences, (3) wants some mutually desirable resource which is in short supply, such that the wants of everyone may not be satisfied fully, and (4) possesses attitudes, values, skills, and goals which are salient in directing one's behavior, but which are perceived to be exclusive of the attitudes, values, skills, and goals held by others(s). Conflict also occurs when two or more social entities (5) have partially exclusive behavioral preferences regarding their joint action, and (6) are interdependent in the performance of their functions or activities. Some of the incidents of conflict behavior are tension, frustration, verbal abuse, annoyance, interference, rivalry, etc.

Threshold of Conflict

Conflict does not necessarily occur simply because there are incompatibilities, disagreements, or differences within or between social entities. In order for conflict to occur, it has to exceed the threshold level of intensity before the parties experience any conflict. In other words, the incompatibilities, disagreements, or differences must be serious enough before the parties experience conflict. There are differences in the threshold of conflict awareness or tolerance among individuals. As a result, some individuals may become involved in a conflict sooner than others under similar situations.

Conflict and Competition

Ambiguity in the distinction between competition and conflict has been a source of confusion (Schmidt & Kochan, 1972). The distinction between these two terms should be delineated in order to understand the nature of conflict. Three major distinctions in the conceptualization of conflict and competition are presented below.

Boulding (1962) considers conflict as a subset of competition which "exists when any potential positions of two behavior units are mutually incompatible .... [Conflict is considered] as a situation of competition in which the parties are *aware* of the incompatibility of potential future positions and in which the party *wishes* to occupy a position that is incompatible with the wishes of the other" (p. 4). According to this conceptualization, all situations of incompatibility lead to competition, but conflict occurs when the parties become aware of the incompatibility and wish to interfere with the attainment of each other's goal attainments. In this sense, golf is a competitive game; football, a conflictual one.

Another possible distinction has been based on whether the behavior of the parties to interaction is regulated by rules and norms. According to Mack (1965), competitive behavior is so regulated, while conflictual behavior is not. Brickman (1974), however, has persuasively argued that the presence or absence of rule structures in conflict situations has little if anything to do with the amount of competition present in conflict.

Conflict and competition may be distinguished neither by the presence or absence of rule structures, nor by anything to do with phenomenology of the interactants. Rather, the distinction may be approached in a manner similar to Rapoport (1960; see also Schelling, 1960), and may be argued that (contrary to Boulding) competition is a subset of conflict. Conflicts may be placed along a continuum of cooperative to competitive, the former occurring when there is a payoff cell or set of cells in which both parties receive satisfactory and high outcomes, and the latter occurring when there only occur joint payoffs such that one party wins and the other loses (cf., Thibaut & Kelley, 1959).

In the language of game theory (e. g., Schelling, 1960), it is possible to both label and diagram three ideal points along this cooperative-competitive continuum to facilitate the categorization of conflicts. Purely cooperative conflicts (technically, "positive-sum games" or "conflicts of coordination") occur in such social situations as a lost child trying to find his or her mother (and vice versa), a subordinate attempting to clarify his assignment with the supervisor, and two parties on the telephone who have been disconnected, trying to reestablish their communication link. The problem is simply one of coordiantion—of establishing who does what in order to insure a mutually profitable outcome for both individuals or units.

Purely competitive conflicts are technically termed "zero-sum games" or "negative-sum games," in which the positive outcomes to one party are directly and equally matched by negative outcomes to the other as a result of their joint choices from interaction. An organizational illustration is that of recruitment, where two candidates are interviewed but only one can be hired.

Of course, in real life and including managerial settings, one hardly encounters *purely* cooperative or purely competitive conflict situations. Rather, most conflicts are characterized by both cooperative and competitive aspects, i.e., they are "non-zero-sum games" or mixed-motive" conflicts. Most managerial conflicts are mixed-motive in nature.

CLASSIFYING CONFLICT

The literature of organizational behavior and management has highlighted different types of conflict. Conflict may be classified on the basis of its source. It may also be classified on the basis of organizational levels, such as individual, group, etc., at which it may originate.

Sources

The classification of conflict is often made on the basis of the antecedent conditions which lead to conflict. Conflict may originate from a number of sources, such as tasks, values, goals, etc. It has been found appropriate to classify conflict on the basis of these sources for proper understanding of its nature and implications. Following is a brief description of this classification.

1. *Affective Conflict* occurs when two interacting social entities become aware that their feelings and emotions are incompatible (Guetzkow & Gyr, 1954).

2. *Conflict of Interest* occurs when two social entities compete for scarce resources. That is, it can be "defined as a discrepancy between them in preferences for outcomes of decisions on the distribution of a scarce resource" (Druckman & Zechmeister, 1973, p. 449). Manager A's and B's contention for the same vice-president's job exemplifies a conflict of interest.

3. *Conflict of Values* occurs when two social entities differ in their values or ideologies on certain issues. Supervisor A's and B's ideological disagreement on the question of "compensatory hiring" is an example of value conflict.

4. *Cognitive Conflict* occurs when two interacting social entities become aware that their thought processes or perceptions are incongruent. "Cognitive conflict between decision makers is the awareness of inconsistent inferences drawn from identical information. In its extreme form, two parties' inferences from the same data are logical contradictions of one another" (Cosier & Rose, 1977, p. 379).

5. *Goal Conflict* occurs when a preferred outcome or an end-state of two social entities is inconsistent. In rare cases "it may involve divergent preferences over all of the decision outcomes, constituting a zero-sum game" (Cosier & Rose 1977, p. 378). Manager A's and B's understanding that only one of their preferred job design programs can be implemented for their division is an example of goal conflict.

6. *Substantive Conflict* occurs when the members of a group disagree on their task or content issues (Guetzkow & Gyr, 1954).

Levels

Organizational conflict may also be classified on the basis of levels (individual, group, etc.) at which it occurs. On this basis organizational conflict may be classified as intrapersonal, interpersonal, intragroup, and intergroup. These four types of conflict may be described as follows:

1. *Intrapersonal Conflict.* This type of conflict is also called intraindividual conflict. It occurs when an organizational member is required to perform certain tasks and roles, which do not match his or her expertise, interests, goals, and values.

2. *Interpersonal Conflict.* This refers to conflict between two or more organizational members of the same or different hierarchical levels or units. The studies on superior-subordinate conflict relate to this type of conflict.

3. *Intergroup Conflict.* This refers to conflict among members of a group, or between two or more subgroups within a group. Such a conflict

may also occur as a result of incompatibilities or disagreements between some or all the members of a group and its leader(s).

4. *Intergroup Conflict.* This refers to conflict between two or more units or groups within an organization. Conflict between line and staff, production and marketing, and headquarters and field staffs are examples of this type of conflict.

Styles

There are various styles of behavior by which interpersonal conflict may be handled. Mary P. Follet (1940) found three main ways of dealing with conflict: domination, compromise, and integration. She also found other ways of handling conflict in organizations, such as avoidance and suppression. Blake and Mouton (1964) first presented a conceptual scheme for classifying the modes (styles) for handling interpersonal conflicts into five types: forcing, withdrawing, smoothing, compromising, and problem solving. They described the five modes of handling conflict on the basis of the attitudes of the manager: concern for production and for people. Their scheme was reinterpreted by Thomas (1976). He considered the intentions of a party (cooperativeness, i.e., attempting to satisfy the other party's concerns; and assertiveness, i.e., attempting to satisfy one's own concerns) in classifying the modes of handling conflict into five types.

Using a conceptualization similar to Blake and Mouton (1964) and Thomas (1976), the styles of handling conflict were differentiated on two basic dimensions, concern for self and for others. The first dimension explains the degree (high or low) to which a person attempts to satisfy his own concern. The second dimension explains the degree (high or low) to which a person wants to satisfy the concern of others. It should be pointed out that these dimensions portray the motivational orientations of a given individual during conflict (Rubin & Brown, 1975). A study by Ruble and Thomas (1976) yielded general support for these dimensions. Combination of the two dimensions results in five specific styles of handling interpersonal conflict, as shown in Figure 2.1 (Rahim & Bonoma, 1979, p. 1327).

The styles of handling interpersonal conflict are described as follows:

1. *Integrating:* high concern for self and others. This involves collaboration between the parties, i.e., openness, exchange of information, and examination of differences to reach a solution acceptable to both parties. "The first rule for obtaining integration is to put your cards on the table, face the real issue, uncover the conflict, bring the whole thing into the open" (Follet, 1940, p. 38).

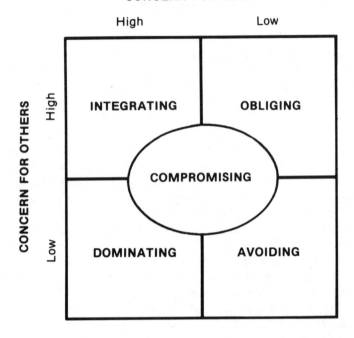

FIGURE 2.1. A Two-Dimensional Model of Styles of Handling Interpersonal Conflict

Prein (1976) suggested that this style has two distinctive elements: confrontation and problem solving. Confrontation involves open and direct communication which should make way for problem solving. As a result, it may lead to creative solutions to problems.

2. *Obliging:* low concern for self and high concern for others. This style is associated with attempting to play down the differences and emphasizing commonalities to satisfy the concern of the other party. There is an element of self-sacrifice in this style. It may take the form of selfless generosity, charity, or obedience to another person's order.

An obliging person neglects his or her own concern to satisfy the concern of the other party. Such an individual is like a "conflict absorber," i.e., a person whose reaction to a perceived hostile act on the part of another has low hostility or even positive friendliness (Boulding, 1962, p. 171).

3. *Dominating:* high concern for self and low concern for others. This style has been identified with win-lose orientation or with forcing behavior to win one's position. A dominating or competing person goes

all out to win his or her objective and, as a result, often ignores the needs and expectations of the other party. Dominating may mean standing up for one's rights and/or defending a position which the party believes to be correct.

Sometimes a dominating person wants to win at any cost. A dominating supervisor is likely to use his position power to impose his will on the subordinates and command their obedience.

4. *Avoiding:* low concern for self and others. It has been associated with withdrawal, buckpassing, sidestepping, or "see no evil, hear no evil, speak no evil" situations. It may take the form of postponing an issue until a better time, or simply withdrawing from a threatening situation. An avoiding person fails to satisfy his or her own concern as well as the concern of the other party.

This style is often characterized as an unconcerned attitude toward the issues or parties involved in conflict. Such a person may refuse to acknowledge in public that there is a conflict which should be dealt with.

5. *Compromising*: intermediate in concern for self and others. It involves give-and-take or sharing whereby both parties give up something to make a mutually acceptable decision. It may mean splitting the difference, exchanging concession, or seeking a quick middle-ground position.

A compromising party gives up more than a dominating but less than an obliging party. Likewise, such a party addresses an issue more directly than an avoiding party, but does not explore it in as much depth as an integrating party.

Additional insights may be gained by reclassifying the five styles of handling interpersonal conflict according to the terminologies of the game theory. Intergrating style can be reclassified to positive-sum (win-win) style, compromising to mixed (no-win/no-lose) style, and obliging, dominating, and avoiding to zero-sum or negative-sum (lose-win, win-lose, and lose-lose, respectively) style. As will be seen in Chapter 5, in general positive-sum, and to some extent mixed, styles are appropriate for dealing with the strategic issues. The zero-sum styles can be used to deal with tactical, day-to-day, or routine problems.

It has been suggested by Thomas (1976) that further insights into the five styles of handling interpersonal conflict may be obtained by organizing them according to the integrative and distributive dimensions of labor-management bargaining suggested by Walton and McKersie (1965). The two dimensions are represented by the broken lines in Figure 2.2.

The integrative dimensions (integrating-avoiding) represents the degree (high or low) of satisfaction of concerns received by self and others. The distributive dimension (dominating-obliging) represents the

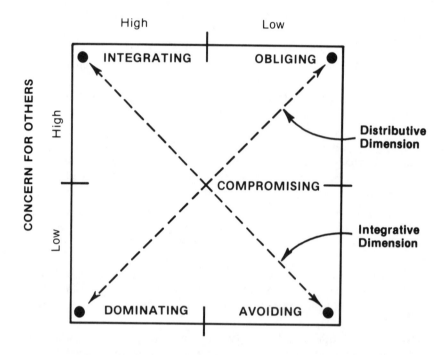

FIGURE 2.2. Integrative and Distributive Dimensions of Styles of Handling Interpersonal Conflict

proportion of the satisfaction of concerns received by self and others. In the integrative dimension, integrating attempts to increase the satisfaction of the concerns of both parties by finding unique solutions to the problems acceptable to them. Avoiding leads to the reduction of satisfaction of the concerns of both parties as a result of their failure to confront and solve their problems. In the distributive dimension, whereas dominating attempts to obtain high satisfaction of concerns for self (and provide low satisfaction of concerns for others), obliging attempts to obtain low satisfaction of concerns for self (and provides high satisfaction of concerns for others). Compromising represents the point of intersection of the two dimensions, i.e., a middle-ground position where each party receives an intermediate level of satisfaction of their concerns from the resolution of their conflicts.

It is generally agreed that the above design for conceptualizing the styles of handling interpersonal conflict is a noteworthy improvement over the simple cooperative-competitive dichotomy suggested by earlier researchers. Further discussions on these five styles of handling interpersonal conflict are continued in Chapters 3 and 5.

SYSTEM PERSPECTIVE

It was indicated in the definition of organizational conflict that conflict may occur within or between social entities. This distinction between conflict *within* and conflict *between* social entities depends upon a system perspective for a given problem. The classification of conflict into four types, based on the level of their origin, shows that analysis at different levels may be beneficial depending on the nature of the problem(s).

SUMMARY

There is no generally accepted definition of conflict. It was defined as an interactive state manifested in disagreements, differences, or incompatibility within or between social entities, i.e., individual, group, and organization. The threshold of conflict indicates that the disagreements or differences between social entities have to be significant or serious enough before the parties engage in conflict. Competition is a part of conflict. Conflict may be placed along a continuum from cooperative conflict to competitive conflict. Cooperative or positive-sum conflict occurs when both parties receive satisfactory outcomes and competitive or zero-sum conflict occurs when one party wins and the other party loses. Most managerial conflicts are characterized by both cooperative and competitive aspects, i.e., mixed motive conflicts.

Conflict can be classified on the basis of the antecedent conditions which lead to conflict. Accordingly, conflict can be classified into six types: affective conflict, conflict of interest, conflict of values, cognitive conflict, goal conflict, and substantive conflict. Conflict can also be classified according to the levels of its origin, such as intrapersonal, interpersonal, intragroup, and intergroup. The styles of handling interpersonal conflict can be classified as integrating, obliging, dominating, avoiding, and compromising. The classification of conflict according to organizational levels shows that an analysis of conflict at different levels can be effective depending on the nature of the problem(s).

The next chapter discusses the overall design or strategy for the management of different types of organizational conflict.

REFERENCES

Blake, R. R., & Mouton, J.S. (1964). *The managerial grid.* Houston, TX.: Gulf Publishing.

Boulding, K. E. (1962). *Conflict and defense: A general theory.* New York: Harper.

Brickman, P. (1974). Rule structure and conflict relationships: Readings in rule structure and conflict relationships. (pp. 1–33) In P. Brickman (Ed.), *Social conflict.* Lexington, Mass: D. C. Heath.

Cosier, R. A., & Rose, G.L. (1977). Cognitive conflict and goal conflict effects on task performance. *Organizational Behavior and Human Performance, 19,* 378 – 391

Druckman, D., & Zechmeister, K. (1973). Conflict of interest and value dissensus: Propositions in the sociology of conflict. *Human Relations, 26,* 449–466.

Fink, C. F. (1968). Some conceptual difficulties in the theory of social conflict. *Journal of Conflict Resolution, 12,* 412–460.

Follet, M. P. (1940). Constructive conflict. In H. C. Metcalf & L. Urwick (Eds.), *Dynamic administration: The collected papers of Mary Parker Follet* (pp. 30–49) New York: Harper. (Originally published, 1926.)

Guetzkow, H., & Gyr, J. (1954). An analysis of conflict in decision-making groups. *Human Relations, 7,* 367–381.

Litterer, J.A. (1966). Conflict in organization: A re-examination. *Academy of Management Journal, 9,* 178–186.

Mack, R. W. (1965). The components of social conflict. *Social Problems, 12,* 388–397.

March, J. G., & Simon, H. A. (1958). *Organizations.* New York: Wiley.

Pondy, L. R.(1967). Organizational conflict: Concepts and models. *Administrative Science Quarterly, 12,* 296–320.

Prein, H. C. M. (1976). Stijlen van conflicthantering. [styles of handling conflict.] *Nederlands Tijdschrift voor de Psychologie, 31,* 321–346.

Rahim, A., & Bonoma, T. V. (1979). Managing organizational conflict: A model for diagnosis and intervention. *Psychological Reports, 44,* 1323–1344.

Rapoport, A. (1960). *Fights, games, and debates.* Ann Arbor: University of Michigan Press.

Ruble, T. L., & Thomas, K. W. (1976). Support for a two-dimensional model for conflict behavior. *Organizational Behavior and Human Performance, 16,* 143–155.

Rubin, J. Z., & Brown, B. R. (1975). *The social psychology of bargaining and negotiation.* New York: Academic Press.

Schelling, T. C. (1960). *The strategy of conflict.* Cambridge, MA.: Harvard University Press.

Schmidt, S. M., & Kochan T. A. (1972). Conflict: Toward conceptual clarity. *Administrative Science Quarterly, 17,* 359–370.

Smith, C. G. (1966). A comparative analysis of some conditions and consequences of intraorganizational conflict. *Administrative Science Quarterly, 10,* 504–529.

Tedeschi, J. T., Schlenker, B. R., & Bonoma, T. V. (1973). *Conflict, power and games: The experimental study of interpersonal relations.* Chicago: Aldine.

Thibaut, J. W., & Kelley, H. H. (1959). *The social psychology of groups.* New York: Wiley.

Thomas. K. W. (1976). Conflict and conflict management. In M. D. Dunnette (Ed.), *Handbook of industrial and organizational psychology* (pp. 889–935). Chicago: Rand McNally.

Walton, R. E., & Dutton, R. B. (1965). *A behavioral theory of labor negotiations: An analysis of a social interaction system.* New York: McGraw-Hill.

3

Conflict Management Design

Even though conflict is often said to be functional for organizations, most recommendations relating to organizational conflict still fall within the realm of conflict resolution, reduction, or minimization. Insofar as it could be determined, the literature on organizational conflict is deficient in two major areas. (1) There is no clear set of rules to suggest when conflict ought to be maintained at a certain level, when reduced, and when ignored. (2) There is no clear set of guidelines to suggest how conflict can be reduced or generated to increase organizational effectiveness. This book attempts to address these issues to develop a design or strategy for managing intrapersonal, interpersonal, intragroup, and intergroup conflicts.

DEFINING CONFLICT MANAGEMENT

It will be evident in this chapter and throughout this book that the emphasis is away from the resolution to management of conflict. The difference is more than semantic (Boulding, 1968, p. 410; Robbins, 1978). Conflict resolution implies reduction or elimination of conflict. The management of different types of organizational conflict involves the following:

1. The management of intrapersonal conflict involves matching the individual goals and role expectations with the needs of the task and role demand in order to optimize the attainment of individual and organizational goals.

2. The management of interpersonal conflict involves enabling the organizational members to learn the five styles of handling conflict so that the different situations can be effectively dealt with.

3. The management of intragroup conflict involves channeling the

energies, expertise, and resources of the group members toward the formulation and/or attainment of group goals.

4. At the intergroup level, conflict management involves channeling the energies, expertise, and resources of the members of conflicting groups for synergistic solutions to their common problems or attainment of overall organizational goals.

The above definitions imply that the management of conflict does not necessarily imply reduction or elimination of conflict. Several researchers have noted the positive consequences of conflict (Assael,1969; Evan, 1965; Hall & Williams, 1966; Janis, 1971; Pelz, 1967). Empirical studies have found that small groups are more productive when dissenters, who create conflict, are present than when there is no difference of opinion or conflict among members (Cartwright & Zander, 1968). Schwenk and Thomas (1983) found in their experimental study that managers who received conflicting analyses came up with higher expected profits than those managers who received single analyses. The studies included by Tjosvold and Johnson in their book indicate that conflict in organizations can be productive if it is handled in a constructive manner.

It was suggested in Chapter 1 that organizations in which there is little or no conflict may stagnate. On the other hand, organizational conflict left uncontrolled may have dysfunctional effects. The consensus among the organization theorists is that a moderate amount of conflict is necessary for attaining an optimum level of job performance. Therefore, it appears that the relationship between the amount of conflict and job performance approximates an inverted-U function. Figure 3.1 shows that a low level of job performance $(OY_1,)$ will be attained when the amount of conflict is low (O) or high (OX_1). At a moderate amount of conflict $(ox,)$ an optimum level of job performance (OY) can be attained. This relationship is expected to hold good when other factors which affect job performance are held constant. (cf., Rahim & Bonoma, 1979, p. 1326).

This is consistent with the activation theory which supports the inverted-U relationship between a person's activation or arousal level and his job performance (Scott, 1966). It is interesting to note that Vroom's (1964, pp. 204–210) reviews of empirical studies indicated that the relationship between the amount of motivation and level of performance is approximated by an inverted-U function. In general, a moderate amount of conflict may provide necessary activation or stimulation in order to optimize job performance of the organizational members or to enhance their adaptive or innovative capabilities. As such, Brown (1983) has suggested that "*conflict management can require intervention to reduce conflict if there is too much, or intervention to promote conflict if there is too little*" (p. 9). As will be seen later, conflict management involves more than just reducing or generating conflict to attain a moderate amount of it.

Argyris (1976, 1980) and Agryris and Schon (1978) have argued that an intervention for managing conflict should promote double-loop rather than single-loop organizational learning. Organizational learning was defined by them as the process of detection and correction of error. "Learning that results in detection and correction of error without changing the underlying policies, assumptions, and goals may be called single-loop. Double-loop learning occurs when the detection and correction of error requires changes in the underlying policies, assumptions, and goals" (Argyris, 1980, p. 291). It should be noted that double-loop organizational learning is quite consistent with the approach to conflict management presented in this book.

A few things should be said about the relationship presented in Figure 3.1. There is no empirical evidence in support of the inverted-U function. Probably there are two major reasons for this lack of evidence. The first is the usual problem of reliable and valid measures of conflict and organizational effectiveness. The second is the problem of isolating the effect of conflict on effectiveness, after controlling for the numerous extraneous independent variables which affect organizational effectiveness. There is no study on this function which has satisfied the requirement of proper control. Several studies on interorganizational conflict in marketing channels found positive as well as negative relationship between conflict and channel performance or efficiency (Reve & Stern, 1979). Pearson and Monoky (1976) found the level of

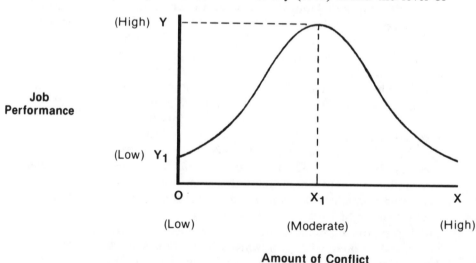

FIGURE 3.1. Relationship between Amount of Conflict and Job Performance

service output to be negatively related to channel conflict. The study by Lusch (1976) found no support for the inverted-U relationship between channel conflict and dealer operating performance. He concluded "that for the distribution of automobiles in the United States (at least for the five channels studied) channel conflict does not have a threshold effect on dealer operating performance" (p. 12). These two and other studies on this relationship have the major limitation of control. Lusch (1976) particularly recognized this problem and concluded that "further research should attempt to control for some of the other variables that influence retailer performance so that the impact of channel conflict can be isolated" (p. 89).

Studies on the management of organizational conflict have taken two directions. Some researches have attempted to measure the amount of conflict at various organizational levels and to explore the sources of such conflict. Implicit in these studies is that a moderate amount of conflict may be maintained for increasing organizational effectiveness by altering the sources of conflict. Others have attempted to relate the various styles of handling interpersonal conflict of the organizational participants and their effects on quality of problem solution or attainment of social system objectives. It becomes evident from this discussion that the distinction between the "amount of conflict" at various levels and the "styles of handling interpersonal conflict," discussed in the previous chapter, is essential for a proper understanding of the nature of conflict management.

The previous discussion was mainly based on the notion of the amount of conflict. In recent years, some researchers have used the indices of annoyance, disputes, distrust, disagreement, incompatibility, etc. to measure conflict at various levels. These are measures of the amount of conflict which are quite distinct from the styles of handling conflict. There are various sources which affect the amount of conflict. The management of conflict partly involves the identification and alteration of these sources to attain and maintain a moderate amount of conflict at each level.

The previous chapter presented the five styles of handling interpersonal conflict, such as integrating, obliging, dominating, avoiding, and compromising. Although some behavioral scientists suggest that integrating or problem-solving style is most appropriate for managing conflict (e.g., Blake & Mouton, 1964; Burke, 1969; Likert & Likert, 1976), it has been indicated by others that, for conflicts to be managed functionally, one style may be more appropriate than another depending upon the situation (Hart, 1981; Rahim & Bonoma, 1979; Thomas, 1977). The situations in which each of the styles is appropriate or inappropriate have been described in Table 3.1 (Rahim, 1983d).

TABLE 3.1. Styles of Handling Interpersonal Conflict and Situations Where They Are Appropriate or Inappropriate

Conflict Style	Situations Where Appropriate	Situations Where Inappropriate
Integrating	1. Issues are complex. 2. Synthesis of ideas is needed to come up with better solutions. 3. Commitment is needed from other parties for successful implementation. 4. Time is available for problem-solving. 5. One party alone cannot solve the problem. 6. Resources possessed by different parties are needed to solve their common problems.	1. Task or problem is simple. 2. Immediate decision is required. 3. Other parties are unconcerned about outcome.
Obliging	1. You believe that you may be wrong. 2. Issue is more important to the other party. 3. You are willing to give up something in exchange for something from the other party in the future. 4. You are dealing from a position of weakness. 5. Preserving relationship is important.	1. Issue is important to you. 2. You believe that you are right. 3. Temporary resolution may provide more time to reach an agreement in the near future.
Dominating	1. Issue is trivial. 2. Speedy decision is needed. 3. Unpopular course of action is implemented.	1. Issue is complex. 2. Issue is not important to you. 3. Both parties are equally powerful.

TABLE 3.1 *(continued)*

Conflict Style	Situations Where Appropriate	Situations Where Inappropriate
	4. Necessary to overcome assertive subordinates.	4. Decision does not have to be made quickly.
	5. Unfavorable decision by the other party may be costly to you.	5. Subordinates possess high degree of competency.
	6. Subordinates lack expertise to make technical decisions.	
	7. Issue is important to you.	
Avoiding	1. Issue is trivial.	1. Issue is important to you.
	2. Potential dysfunctional effect of confronting the other party outweights benefits of resolution.	2. It is your responsibility to make decision.
	3. Cooling off period is needed.	3. Parties are unwilling to defer, issue must be resolved.
		4. Prompt attention is needed.
Compromising	1. Goals of parties are mutually exclusive.	1. One party is more powerful.
	2. Parties are equally powerful.	2. Problem is complex enough needing problem-solving approach.
	3. Consensus cannot be reached.	
	4. Integrating or dominating style is not successful.	
	5. Temporary solution to a complex problem is needed.	

In general, integrating and, to some extent compromising, styles are appropriate for dealing with the strategic issues. The remaining styles can be used to deal with tactical or day-to-day problems. The above discussion on the styles of handling conflict and the situations where they are appropriate or inappropriate is a normative approach to managing conflict.

Up to this point it has been argued that the management of conflict not only refers to maintaining a moderate amount of conflict but also handling the same through appropriate styles of behavior. The organizational literature has failed to integrate these two approaches which are not mutually exclusive. To make conflict management effective both approaches may be used simultaneously. In other words, a moderate amount of conflict may be maintained by altering the sources of conflict and the organizational participants may be trained to learn the various behavioral styles for effectively handling their interpersonal conflict in different situations.

ORGANIZATIONAL EFFECTIVENESS

Previous discussion has made several references to organizational effectivenss. It was suggested that a moderate amount of conflict is necessary to maximize organizational effectivensss. It was also suggested that organizational participants must learn the five styles of handling conflict to deal with different conflict situations effectively. In other words, if the variables other than conflict, which affect organizational effectiveness, are controlled, effectiveness can be maximized if a moderate amount of conflict is maintained and organizational members use different styles of handling conflict depending on situations. This indicates that the management of organizational conflict requires proper understanding of the effect of conflict on organizational effectiveness. Goodman and Pinnings (1977) have argued that effectiveness is the central theme in organizational analysis and it is difficult to conceive of an organization theory that does not include the construct of effectiveness.

The literature on organizational behavior implicitly or explicitly suggests that organizational processes or conditions, such as leadership, conflict, communication, structure, technology, etc., influence the effectiveness of an organization. This implies that organizational effectiveness can be conceptualized and measured. It may come as a surprise that researchers have given inadequate attention to this problem. Most of the recent textbooks on organizational behavior do not contain any systematic discussion on organizational effectiveness. Content analysis of syllabi on organizational behavior courses for MBA students indicated that organizational effectiveness was the thirty-first among the sixty-five frequently mentioned topics (Rahim, 1981).

The literature shows that there is little agreement regarding the conceptualization and measurement of this factor (Steers, 1977). It is generally agreed that the literature on organizational effectiveness is in disarray (Quinn & Rohrbaugh, 1983).

There are two basic models of organizational effectiveness: goal attainment and systems models. Whereas the goal attainment model attempts to assess organizational effectiveness in terms of the *ends*, the systems model focuses on the *means* for the achievement.

Goal Attainment Model

According to this model, the effectiveness of an organization is assessed in terms of ends as opposed to means. One of the advocates of this model is Etzioni (1964) who defined organizational effectiveness as the ability of a social system to achieve its goals or objectives. The measures of goal attainment very often take the form of productivity or efficiency. Another common measure of goal attainment is profitability or return on investment.

Apparently the measures of goal attainment appear to be simple, but the goals of complex organizations range far beyond output or profitability. One of the major criticisms of this approach relates to the difficulty in identifying the goals of an organization. Another problem is the unavailability of goal attainment measures, such as profitability, for nonprofit organizations.

System Resource Model

Yuchtman and Seashore (1967) have proposed a "system resource" approach to organizational effectiveness which builds on Katz and Kahn's (1966) view about organizations. This model has received widespread attention in organizational effectiveness literature. This approach is concerned with an organization's ability to secure an advantageous bargaining position in its environment to obtain scarce and valued resources. By "bargaining position" the writers meant "the exclusion of any specific goal (or function) as the ultimate criterion of organizational effectiveness. Instead it points to the more general capacity of the organization as a resource-getting system" (Yuchtman & Seashore, 1967, p. 898).

The system resource model by Yuchtman and Seashore (1967) has been criticized by Hall (1977) and others, who pointed out that this typology of effectiveness may in large measure represent an argument over semantics. As Hall (1977) points out, "the acquisition of resources does not just happen. It is based on what the organization is trying to achieve—its goal—but it is accomplished through the operative goals" (p. 91).

Although it has been argued that the goal-attainment and systems approaches to organizational effectiveness are incompatible, the two can be complementary. The conceptualization of organizational effectiveness must consider not only the goals of an organization, but also the processes through which it attains its objectives (Steers, 1977). Although two models have been presented here other models have been suggested by researchers in an attempt to integrate the literature (e.g., Cameron, 1978; Scott, 1977). It is beyond the scope of this chapter to discuss and integrate these models.

Measurement of Effectiveness

A recent literature review by Campbell (1977) found that over thirty different criteria were used for the measurement of organizational effectiveness. These measurement criteria ranged from global to specific aspects of organizational effectiveness. It also becomes evident that some of the measurement criteria are inconsistent, i.e., an organization cannot attempt to satisfy several of these effectiveness criteria simultaneously. The review revealed that few studies used multivariate measures of effectiveness and the same criteria were hardly used across studies.

Steers (1975) reviewed a representative sample of seventeen studies which used multivariate models of organizational effectiveness and found no convergence on a set of measures of organizational effectiveness. Only one criterion, adaptability-flexibility, was mentioned frequently in these models, followed by productivity, satisfaction, profitability, and resource acquisition. An organizational analyst must decide the dimensions of organizational effectiveness which must be measured and the method of data collection to be used.

PROCESS OF MANAGING CONFLICT

The management of organizational conflict involves the process of diagnosis and intervention in conflict. Diagnosis provides the basis for intervention. This process is shown in Figure 3.2.

Diagnosis

Following Levinson (1972) identification or diagnosis of the problems of conflict in an organization must precede any intervention designed to manage the conflict. DuBrin (1972; see also Brown, 1979) specifically suggested the need for the diagnosis of intergroup conflict through some formal and informal approaches. Proper diagnosis of the

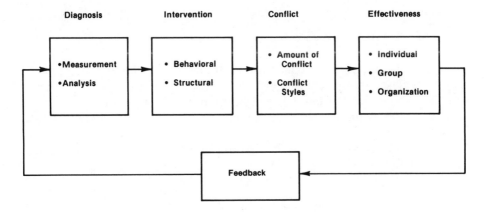

FIGURE 3.2. Process of Managing Organizational Conflict

causes of conflicts in a system is important because the underlying causes of conflicts may not be what they appear on the surface. If an intervention is made without a proper diagnosis of conflict, then there is the probability that a change agent may try to solve a wrong problem. This will lead to what Mitroff and Featheringham (1974) call the error of the third kind. This error has been defined by them "as the probability of having solved the wrong problem when one should have solved the right problem" (p. 383). The management of organizational conflict involves a systematic diagnosis of the problems in order to minimize the error of the third kind. The diagnostic aspect of conflict management has been particularly neglected by the management researchers and practitioners. The diagnosis involves measurement of conflict, its sources, and effectiveness, and analysis of relations among them.

Measurement

A comprehensive diagnosis involves the measurement as follows:

1. The amount of intrapersonal, intragroup, and intergroup conflicts.
2. The styles of handling interpersonal conflict of the organizational members with superior(s), subordinates, and peers.
3. The sources of (1) and (2).
4. Individual, group, and organizational effectiveness.

Analysis

The analysis of data collected above should include:

1. The amount of conflict and the styles of handling conflict classified by departments, units, divisions, etc. and whether they are different from their corresponding national norms.
2. The relationships of the amount of conflict, conflict styles, and their sources.
3. The relationships of the amount of conflict, conflict styles, and effectiveness.

The results of diagnosis should indicate whether there is any need for and the type of intervention necessary for managing conflict. The results of diagnosis should be discussed preferably by a representative group of managers, who are concerned with the management of conflict, with the help of an outside expert who specializes in conflict research and training. A discussion of the results should enable the managers to identify the problems of conflict, if any, that should be resolved.

The above discussion presented an approach that may be used to conduct a comprehensive diagnosis of conflict. This should not be taken to mean that every organization requires such a diagnosis. A management practitioner or consultant should decide when and to what extent a diagnosis is needed for a proper understanding of a conflict problem.

Recently, two instruments were designed by the author for measuring the amount of conflict at individual, group, and intergroup levels, and the five styles of handling interpersonal conflict. The Rahim Organizational Conflict Inventory-I (ROCI-I) was designed to measure intrapersonal, intragroup, and intergroup conflicts (Rahim, 1983b). The ROCI-I uses self-report to measure intrapersonal conflict and perceptions of organizational memebers to measure the amount of intragroup and intergroup conflicts. The Rahim Organizational Confict Inventory-II (ROCI-II) uses self-reports for measuring the styles of handling interpersonal conflict of an organizational member with his or her superior (s) (Form A), subordinates (Form B), and peers (Form C) (Rahim, 1983c). These instruments use a 5-point Likert scale to measure the amount of conflict at the three levels and the five styles of handling interpersonal conflict. A higher score represents perception of a greater amount of one type of conflict or more use of a conflict style. The test-retest and internal consistency reliabilities and construct and empirical validities of the scale of the two instruments were found to be adequate (Rahim, 1983a,d,e). The ROCI-I and ROCI-II were used to collect data from two random national samples of 1,188 and 1,219 executives, respectively. The percentile and reference group norms of the three types of conflict and the styles of handling interpersonal conflict have been reported in Chapters 4 through 7.

Data collected through the questionnaires should not be the sole basis of a diagnosis. In-depth interviews with the conflicting parties and observation may be needed to gain a better understanding of the nature of conflict and the type of intervention needed.

Intervention

A proper diagnosis should indicate whether there is any need for intervention and the type of intervention required. An intervention may be needed if there is too little or too much conflict and/or the organizational members are not handling their conflict effectively. The national norms of conflict reported in the following four chapters can provide some rough guidelines to decide whether an organization has too little or too much of a particular type of conflict. In addition to the national norms, data from in-depth interviews are needed to determine the effectiveness of the styles of handling interpersonal conflict of the organizational members. There are two basic approaches to intervention in conflict: behavioral and structural (Rahim, 1977; Rahim & Bonoma, 1979).

Behavioral Approach

The behavioral approach attempts to improve organizational effectiveness by changing members' culture: attitudes, values, norms, beliefs, etc. The behavioral approach is mainly designed to manage conflict by enabling the organizational participants to learn the uses of various styles of handling interpersonal conflict and the situations where they are appropriate or inappropriate.

Applied behavioral scientists have developed organizational development strategies and techniques for improving the organizational efficiency (Bennis, 1969; French & Bell, 1978; Margulise & Raia, 1972), which may be adapted for managing organizational conflict. Traditionally, the theorists of conflict resolution emphasized the areas of agreement of commonality existing between conflicting entities by supression or avoidance of the areas of disagreement. Behavioral and organizational development interventions, on the contrary, are designed to help the organizational participants to learn mainly the integrative or collaborative style of behavior through which to find the "real" causes of the conflict and arrive at functional solutions. Organizational development strategies are especially useful in managing strategic conflict where integrating style is more appropriate than other styles. The classical approach to conflict management which emphasizes obliging, dominating, and avoiding styles may be appropriate when conflict is minor or frictional in nature.

Structural Approach

The structural approach attempts to improve the organizational effectiveness by changing the organization's structural design characteristics: differentiation and integration mechanisms, system of communication, reward structure, etc. This approach mainly attempts to manage conflict by altering the amount of conflict experienced by the organizational participants at various levels.

Conflicts which result from the organization's structural design can be managed effectively by appropriate change in organizational design. Recent research on organization design shows that there is no one best design for all organizations. Whether a mechanistic (bureaucratic) or organic design is appropriate for an organization or one or more of its subsystems depends on situations. There is a growing evidence that the design of an organization should depend on the nature of task or technology (Lawrence & Lorsch, 1967; Perrow, 1967; Rice, 1963; Woodward, 1965) and motivational tendencies of the organizational or subsystem members (Morse & Lorsch, 1970). The greater the congruence among these factors, the more effective is the management of conflict and the greater is the job performance. There are other structural factors, such as reward systems, rules and procedures, nature of tasks, etc., which can be altered to reduce or increase conflict.

An organizational consultant may decide to use both behavioral and structural intervention approaches for managing conflict. It should be noted that although behavioral intervention is primarily designed to alter the styles of handling conflict by changing the culture of the group members, such an intervention may also affect the amount of conflict. On the other hand, the structural intervention is primarily designed to alter the amount of conflict by changing the structural sources of conflict, such an intervention may also affect the styles of handling conflict.

SUMMARY

Organizational conflict must not necessarily be reduced, suppressed, or eliminated, but managed. The management of conflict at the individual, group, and intergroup levels involves the maintenance of a moderate amount of conflict at each level and helping the organizational participants to learn the various styles of handling interpersonal conflict for dealing with different conflict situations effectively.

The relationship between conflict and job performance approximates an inverted-U function. But hard evidence of this function is not yet available. The studies of organizational conflict have taken two directions. One group of studies used the measures of the amount of conflict. Implicit in these studies is that a moderate amount of conflict may be attained by altering the sources of conflict. Other studies have looked at the various styles of handling conflict of the organization members, such as integrating, obliging, dominating, avoiding, and compromising. For conflicts to be managed functionally, one style may be more appropriate than another depending upon the situation.

The management of organizational conflict requires proper understanding of the effects of conflict on organizational effectiveness. There are two major models of organizational effectiveness: goal attainment and systems models. The goal attainment model attempts to assess the effectiveness in terms of the goals of the organization. The systems model focuses on the means to the attainment of goals. Over thirty criteria were used in the measures of organizational effectiveness. One criterion, adaptability-flexibility, was mentioned more frequently, followed by productivity, satisfaction, profitability, and resource acquisition.

The management of organizational conflict involves diagnosis and intervention. A proper diagnosis should include the measures of the amount of conflict, the styles of handling interpersonal conflict, sources of conflict, and effectiveness. It should also indicate the relationship between the amount of conflict and conflict styles and their sources and effectiveness.

Intervention is needed if there is too little or too much conflict and interpersonal conflicts are not handled effectively to deal with different situations. There are two types of intervention: behavioral and structural. The behavioral approach is mainly designed to manage conflict by enabling organizational participants to learn the various styles of handling conflict and their appropriate uses. The structural approach is mainly designed to manage conflict by changing the organization's structural design characteristics. A structural intervention aims mainly at attaining and maintaining a moderate amount of conflict by altering the sources of conflict.

REFERENCES

Argyris, C. (1976). Single-loop and double-loop models in research on decision making. *Administrative Science Quarterly, 21*, 363–375.

Argyris, C. (1980). Some limitations of the case method: Experiences in a management develpoment program. *Academy of Management Review, 5*, 291–298.

Argyris, C., & Schön, D. A. (1978). *Organizational learning: A theory of action perspective*. Reading, MA.: Addison-Wesley.

Assael, H. (1969). Constructive role of interorganizational conflict. *Administrative Science Quarterly, 14*, 573–582.

Bennis, W. G. (1969). *Organization development: Its nature, origins, and prospects*. Reading, MA.: Addison-Wesley.

Blake, R. R., & Mouton, J. S. (1964). *The managerial grid*. Houston, TX.: Gulf Publishing.

Boulding, K. E. Preface to a special issue. *Journal of Conflict Resolution, 12*, 409–411.

Brown, L. D. (1979). Managing conflict among groups. In D. A. Kolb, I. M. Rubin, & J. M. McIntyre (Eds.), *Organizational psychology: A book of readings* (3rd ed.) (377–389) Englewood Cliffs, N.J.: Prentice-Hall.

Brown, L. D. (1983). *Managing conflict at organizational interfaces*. Reading, MA.: Addison-Wesley.

Burke, R. J. (1969). Methods of resolving interpersonal conflict. *Personnel Administration, 32*, (4), 48–55.

Cameron, K. (1978). Measuring organizational effectiveness in institutions of higher education. *Administrative Science Quarterly, 23*, 604–632.

Campbell, J. P. (1977). On the nature of organizational effectiveness. In P. S. Goodman, & J. M. Pennings (Eds.), *New perspectives of organization effectiveness*. San Francisco: Jossey-Bass.

Cartwright, D., & Zander, A. (Eds.). (1968). *Group dynamics: Research and theory* (3rd ed.). New York: Harper & Row.

DuBrin, A. J. (1972). *The practice of managerial psychology: Concepts and methods of manager and organization development* (pp. 211–227). New York: Pergamon Press.

Etzioni, A. (1964). *Modern organizations*. Englewood Cliffs, N.J.: Prentice-Hall.

Evan, W. M. (1965). Conflict and performance in R&D organizations: Some preliminary findings. *Industrial Management Review, 7* (1), 37–46.

French, W. L., & Bell, C. H. (1978). *Organization development*. Englewood Cliffs, N.J.: Prentice-Hall.

Goodman, P. S., & Pinnings, J. M. (Eds.). (1977). *New perspectives on organizational effectiveness*. San Francisco: Jossey-Bass.

Hall, R. H. (1977). *Organizations: Structure and processes*. Englewood Cliffs, N.J.: Prentice-Hall.

Hall, J., & Williams, M. S. (1966). A comparison of decision-making performances in established and ad-hoc groups. *Journal of Personality and Social Psychology, 3*, 214–222.

Hart, L. B. (1971). *Learning from conflict: A handbook for trainers and group leaders*. Reading, MA.: Addison-Wesley.

Janis, I. J. (1971). Groupthink. *Psychology Today*, pp. 43–44, 46, 74–76.

Katz, D., & Kahn, R. L. (1966). *The social psychology of organizations*. New York: Wiley.

Lawrence, P. R., & Lorsch, J. W. (1967). Differentiation and integration in complex organizations. *Administrative Science Quarterly, 12*, 1–47.

Levinson, H. (1972). The clinical psychologist as organizational diagnostician. *Professional Psychology, 3*, 34–40.

Lusch, R. F. (1976). Channel conflict: Its impact on retailer operating performance. *Journal of Retailing, 52* (2), 3–12, 89–90.

Margulies, N., & Raia, A. P (Eds.). (1972). *Organizational development: Values, process, and technology.* New York: McGraw-Hill.

Mitroff, I. I., & Featheringham, T. R. (1974). On systemic problem solving and the error of the third kind. *Behavioral Science, 19*, 383–393.

Morse, J. J., & Lorsch, J. W. (1970). Beyond theory Y. *Harvard Business Review, 48* (3), 61–68.

Pearson, M, & Monoky, J. F. (1976). The role of conflict and cooperation in channel performance. In K. L. Bernhardt (Ed.), *Marketing: 1776–1976 and Beyond.* Chicago: American Marketing Association, (pp. 240–244).

Pelz, D. C. (1967). Creative tensions in the research and development climate. *Science, 157*, 160–165.

Perrow, C. (1967). A framework for comparative organizational analysis. *American Sociological Review, 32*, 194–208.

Quinn, R. E., & Rohrbaugh, J. (1983). A spatial model of effectiveness criteria: Towards a competing values approach to organizational analysis. *Management Science, 29*, 363–377.

Rahim, A. (1977). The management of organizational intergroup conflict: A contingency model. *Proceedings of the 8th Annual Meeting of the Midwest American Institute for Decision Sciences*, Cleveland, OH. , pp. 247–249.

Rahim, A (1981). Organizational behavior courses for graduate students in business administration: Views from the tower and battlefield. *Psychological Reports, 49*, 583–592.

Rahim, M. A. (1983a). A measure of styles of handling interpersonal conflict. *Academy of Management Journal, 26*, 368–376.

Rahim, M. A. (1983b). *Rahim organizational conflict inventory-I.* Palo Alto, CA.: Consulting Psychologists Press.

Rahim, M. A. (1983c). *Rahim organizational conflict inventory-II, Forms, A, B, & C.* Palo Alto, CA.: Consulting Psychologists Press.

Rahim, M. A. (1983d). *Rahim organizational conflict inventories: Professional manual.* Palo Alto, CA.: Consulting Psychologists Press.

Rahim, M. A. (1983e). Measurement of organizational conflict. *Journal of General Psychology, 190*, 189–199.

Rahim, A., & Bonoma, T. V. (1979). Managing organizational conflict: A model for diagnosis and intervention. *Psychological Reports, 44*, 1323–1344.

Reve, T., & Stern, L. W. (1979). Interorganizational relations in marketing channels. *Academy of Management Review, 4*, 405–416.

Rice, A. K. (1963). *The enterprise and its environment: A system theory of management organization.* London: Tavistock.

Robbins, S. P. (1978). "Conflict management" and "conflict resolution" are not synonymous terms. *California Management Review, 21*(2), 67–75.

Schwenk, C. R., & Thomas, H. (1983). Effects of conflicting analyses on managerial decision making: A laboratory experiment. *Decision Sciences, 14,* 467–482.

Scott, W. E. (1966). Activation theory and task design. *Organizational Behavior and Human Performance, 1,* 3–30.

Scott, W. R. (1977). Effectiveness of organizational effectiveness studies. In P. S. Goodman & J. M. Pinnings (Eds.), *New perspectives on organizational effectiveness.* San Francisco: Jossey-Bass.

Steers, R. M. (1975). Problems in the measurement of organizational effectiveness. *Administrative Science Quarterly, 20,* 546–558.

Steers, R. M. (1977). *Organizational effectiveness: A behavioral view.* Santa Monica, CA.: Goodyear.

Thomas, K. W. (1977). Toward multi-dimensional values in teaching: The example of conflict behaviors. *Academy of Management Review, 2,* 484–490.

Tjosvold. D., & Johnson, D. W. (1983). *Productive conflict management: Perspectives for organizations.* New York: Irvington Publishers.

Vroom, V. H. (1964). *Work and motivation.* New York: Wiley.

Woodward, J. (1965). *Industrial organization: Theory and practice.* London: Oxford University Press.

Yuchtman, E., & Seashore, S. E. (1967). A system resource approach to organizational effectiveness. *American Sociological Review, 32,* 891–903.

4

Intrapersonal Conflict

In Chapter 2 conflict was classified as intrapersonal, interpersonal, intragroup, and intergroup. This chapter describes the nature, dynamics, sources, and management of intrapersonal conflict.

Psychologists have studied conflict at the intrapersonal level extensively. They define conflict as "a situation in which a person is motivated to engage in two or more mutually exclusive activities" (Murray, 1968, p. 220). An individual is in an intrapersonal conflict if he has difficulty making a choice because he is pushed or pulled in opposite directions, i.e., the alternatives are both attractive or unattractve. Kurt Lewin's (1948) field theory falls in this category. Lewin conceptualized conflict as a situation where oppositely directed, simultaneous forces of about equal strength occur in a person. The three types of this conflict are defined below.

1. *Approach-Approach Conflict.* This occurs when a person has to choose between two alternatives both of which are attractive. A manager is confronted with an approach-approach conflict if he has to recommend one of the two subordinates for promotion who are equally competent for the position.

2. *Approach-Avoidance Conflict.* This occurs when a person has to deal with a situation which possesses both positive as well as negative aspects, i.e., when a person feels similar degrees of attraction and repulsion toward a goal or competing goals. A faculty member may be in this type of conflict if he wants to joint a top school where the prospect of tenure is uncertain.

3. *Avoidance-Avoidance Conflict.* This conflict occurs when each of the competing alternatives possesses negative consequences, i.e., they are

equally repulsive. A manager will be in this type of conflict if he has to decide between accepting a salary cut for himself or quitting his job. The person is possibly distressed in his attempt to decide upon the lesser of the two evils.

Perceived incompatibilities or incongruencies frequently occur when an organizational participant is required to perform a task which does not match her or his expertise, interests, goals, and values. Such a conflict also occurs if there is a significant mismatch between the role that a person expects to perform and the role that is demanded of the person by the organization. The latter has been classified as role conflict by some researchers (e.g., Kahn, Wolfe, Quinn, Snoak, & Rosenthal, 1964; Rizzo, House, & Lirtzman, 1970). For our purposes role conflict is a part of intrapersonal conflict.

The concepts of role and role conflict have been developed by researchers in several disciplines. Since a number of studies have been conducted on role conflict, a considerable part of this chapter has been devoted to the explanation of the nature of role and role conflict.

ROLE

Common to most definitions of role is the view that an individual behaves with reference to the expectations which others have about the way he should behave. Sarbin (1968, p. 564) defines role as a term generally "used to represent behavior expected of the occupant of a given position or status," while Conway and Feigert (1976, p. 189) suggest at least three uses of the term: First, role is used to mean the attitudes, values, and behavior ascribed by society to persons occupying a given status. Second, role is used to mean an individual's definition of his situation with reference to his and others' societal positions. And third, role is used to refer to the behavior of an individual occupying a social position.

ROLE CONFLICT

Role conflict exists when "situations are so ordered that an actor is required to fill simultaneously two or more roles that present inconsistent, contradictory, or even mutually exclusive expectations" (Getzels & Guba, 1952, p. 165). Kahn et al. (1964) conducted a national study on role conflict and ambiguity. The study involved a survey of 725 subjects representing the labor force of the United States during 1961, and an intensive series of case studies of 53 subjects selected from 6 industrial locations. They defined role conflict as, " the simultaneous occurence of two (or more) sets of pressures such that compliance with one would make more difficult compliance with the other" (p. 19). Kahn et al. identified four distinct types of role conflict.

1. *Intrasender Conflict.* This type of conflict occurs when a role sender requires a role receiver (i.e., the focal person) to perform roles which are contradictory or inconsistent. For example, a role sender may request the role receiver to do something which cannot be done without violating a rule, yet the role sender attempts to enforce the rule.

2. *Intersender Conflict.* The role receiver will experience conflict if the role behavior demanded by one role sender is at odds with the role behavior demanded by another role sender(s). A person who often experiences role conflict is the foreman, who receives instruction from the general foreman which may be inconsistent with the needs and expectations of the workers under the former.

3. *Interrole Conflict.* This type of conflict occurs when an individual occupies two or more roles whose expectations are inconsistent. A corporation president is expected, in that role, to take part in social engagements to promote the image of the corporation. This may be in conflict with his role as a father in which he is expected to spend more time with his children to be an ideal parent.

4. *Intrarole (Person-Role) Conflict.* This type of role conflict occurs when an employee is required to violate moral or ethical values. For example, intrarole conflict occurs when a manager is required to enter into price-fixing conspiracies which are not congruent with his or her ethical standards.

These four types of role conflict may lead to another complex form of conflict called *role overload.* This occurs when an organizational member is required to perform a number of legitimate and compatible roles sent by different role senders, which taken as a set is too much to be accomplished. As a result, the member may set up priorities and perform the roles which he considers more important than others. Role overload is quite prevalent in industry. It "involves a kind of person-role conflict and is perhaps best regarded as a complex, emergent type combining aspects of inter-sender and person-role conflicts" (Kahn et al., 1964, p. 20).

A number of studies on organizational behavior have used role conflict as a univariate construct. Miles and Perreault (1976) suggested the need for studying role conflict as a multivariate construct consisting of various types of conflict discussed before. This is needed to gain proper understanding of the factors which affect different types of role conflict and the effects of such conflicts on individual and organizational effectiveness.

A MODEL OF ROLE CONFLICT AND AMBIGUITY

Figure 4.1 portrays a slightly modified version of Kahn et al.'s (1964, p. 30) model of role conflict and ambiguity. The model can be used to present the notion of role episode and the factors which are involved in adjustment to role conflict and ambiguity.

The model presents role conflict through a series of events or a *role episode*. There are two boxes in the figure, one headed, "role senders" and the other "focal person." The role sender communicates his expectations or influence to the focal person to reinforce or modify his behavior. The box on the left represents the expectations of the role senders (Section I) and the means by which these are communicated (Section II). The box on the right represents the perception of these communications by the focal person (Section III) and his or her response to the influence attempt (Section IV).

The figure illustrates that the episode begins with the role sender's expectations, i.e., the perceptions and evaluations of the focal person's role behavior. He then moves into the next phase (i.e., sent role), which takes the form of role pressure communicated to the focal person. The direction of the arrow between sent role and received role indicates the communication flow from the role sender(s) to the focal person.

The focal person receives the sent role and begins an interpretation process. Role conflict occurs at this stage if the sent role is different from the role expected by the focal person. The next phase is the role behavior, i.e., the response by focal person which may take the form of either compliance or noncompliance with the sent role. The loop connecting the focal person and role sender indicates the feedback mechanism through which the role sender knows how much of the focal person's response is consistent with the sent role. This becomes an input to the process by which the role sender indicates another cycle of role sendings.

The direction of arrows in the broken lines connecting the three circles and the episode indicates that organizational factors (A) may affect an episode. The personality factors (B) of the role senders and the focal person and the interpersonal relations (C) between them may affect an episode as well as be affected by it. Some of the major factors which affect role conflict have been discussed in detail under the heading "sources" of intrapersonal conflict.

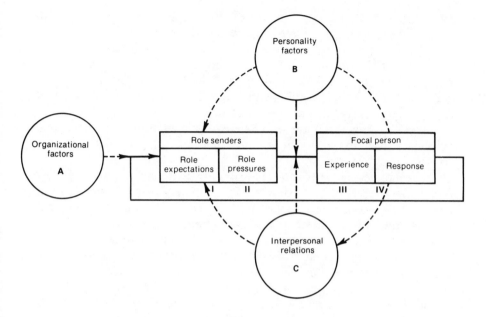

FIGURE 4.1. A Model of Role Conflict and Ambiguity

ROLE AMBIGUITY

A concept closely related to role conflict is role ambiguity. It refers to the lack of clarity in understanding what expectations or prescriptions exist for a given role. An organizational member requires information about the expectations from his role, the means of achieving his role, and consequences of performing his role. Role ambiguity occurs when the information either does not exist or is not properly communicated if it does exist (Kahn et al., 1964).

CONSEQUENCES OF ROLE CONFLICT

A number of studies have attempted to relate role conflict with personal and organizational outcomes. Role conflict has been found to be positively related to job dissatisfaction, tension and anxiety, propensity to leave, lack of confidence in the organization, and inability to influence decision making (Brief & Aldag, 1976; Greene & Organ, 1973; Hamner & Tosi, 1974; House & Rizzo, 1972; Ivancevich & Donnelly, 1974; Johnson & Stinson, 1975; Kahn et al., 1964; Lyons, 1971; Miles,

1975; Miles & Perreault, 1976; Rizzo, House, & Lirtzman, 1970; Tosi, 1971). Sales (1969) investigated the consequences of role overload and found that it can contribute to the cause of coronary disease.

Kahn et al. concluded from their study that "the emotional costs of role conflict for the focal person include low job satisfaction, low confidence in the organization, and a high degree of job-related tension. A very frequent behavioral response to role conflict is withdrawl or avoidance of those who are seen as creating the conflict" (p. 380). Role ambiguity was found to be as prevalent as role conflict, and the consequences are similar.

The studies reported above deal only with the negative or dysfunctional aspects of role conflict. Unfortunately these studies did not attempt to investigate the functional aspects of role conflict which can enhance individual and/or organizational effectiveness. Implicit in the above studies is the notion that role conflict is dysfunctional and should be reduced or eliminated. Although several studies have found adverse effects of role perceptions on a number of attitudinal, behavioral, and psychosomatic outcomes, the relationship between role conflict and organizational effectiveness has yet to be established. Two major problems are associated with the studies on role conflict and organizational effectiveness. These are the failure to control the factors, other than role conflict, which affect organizational effectiveness, and the failure to develop valid measures of organizational effectiveness. As it was emphasized in Chapter 3, organizational conflict of any type must not necessarily be reduced or eliminated but managed to increase organizational effectiveness. The next section deals with this important issue.

MANAGING INTRAPERSONAL CONFLICT

The management of intrapersonal conflict involves matching the individual goals and role expectations with the needs of the task and role demand in order to optimize the attainment of individual and organizational goals. It was suggested in Chapter 3 that the management of conflict involves diagnosis of and intervention in conflict. Following is a discussion on the diagnosis of and intervention in intrapersonal conflict.

Diagnosis

The diagnosis of intrapersonal conflict can be performed by self-report, observation, and interview methods. The ROCI-I uses self-report to measure intrapersonal conflict of organizational members. Rizzo,

House, and Lirtzman (1970) designed a questionnaire to measure role conflict and role ambiguity which is frequently used in organizational studies. They used the self-report of incompatibility inconsistency in the requirements of the role of an individual to measure role conflict and ambiguity. A comprehensive diagnosis of intrapersonal conflict involves the *measurement* as follows:

1. The amount of intrapersonal conflict.
2. The sources of such conflict.
3. The effectiveness of the individual members of an organization.

An *analysis* of the above diagnostic data should be performed to derive the following:

1. The amount of intrapersonal conflict existing in various organizational levels, units, departments, or divisions, and whether they deviated from the national norms significantly.
2. Relationship between intrapersonal conflict and its sources.
3. Relationship between intrapersonal conflict and individual effectiveness.

National Norms

Data for the national norms of intrapersonal, intragroup, and intergroup conflicts were derived from a study conducted to test the reliability and validity of the ROCI-I (Rahim, 1983). In this study the ROCI-I was sent to 4,000 executives randomly selected from the Penton/IPC list of 1.3 million organizational members. These members represented 25 different industries. A cover letter explaining the purpose of the study accompanied the instrument. Usable responses were received from 1,188 executives, a response rate of about 30 percent. Although the response rate was only moderately satisfactory, a follow-up letter was not sent because funds were limited. Tables 4.1 and 4.2 were prepared on the basis of this sample, mentioned in Chapter 3.

Table 4.1 shows the national percentile norms of managers. The percentile score of an individual shows his or her relative position on the intrapersonal conflict scale compared with other members in the normative group. For instance, a subject scoring at 65th percentile on this scale is as high or higher than 65 percent of the normative group. His or her score is exceeded by only 35 percent of this group.

Table 4.2 shows the sample size (N), means (M) (reference group norms), standard deviations (SD) of intrapersonal conflict, classified by

TABLE 4.1. Managerial Percentile Norms of Intrapersonal Conflict ($N = 1,188$)

Mean Scores	Percentiles	Mean Scores
5.00		5.00
4.85		4.85
4.70		4.70
4.55		4.55
4.40		4.40
4.25		4.25
4.10	99	4.10
3.95	98	3.95
3.80	97	3.80
3.65	96	3.65
3.50	95	3.50
3.35	93	3.35
3.20	91	3.20
3.05	89	3.05
2.90	86	2.90
2.75	82	2.75
2.60	77	2.60
2.45	71	2.45
2.30	62	2.30
2.15	53	2.15
2.00	44	2.00
1.85	32	1.85
1.70	23	1.70
1.55	17	1.55
1.40	11	1.40
1.25	7	1.25
1.10	4	1.10
1.00	2	1.00

organizational level, functional area, and education, and the results of one-way analyses of variance (F). The results of one-way analyses of variance show that there were differences in intrapersonal conflict among the executives of top, middle, and lower organizational levels. There was an inverse relationship between organizational level and intrapersonal conflict. There were also some differences in intrapersonal conflict among executives of different functional area. There were no significant differences in conflict among the executives with different educational level.

The normative data should enable a management practitioner or a behavioral science consultant to decide whether the members of an

TABLE 4.2. Managerial Reference Group Norms of Intrapersonal Conflict ($N = 1,188$)

Variables	N	M	SD	F
Organizational Level				69.77*
Top	196	1.86	.5619	
Middle	407	2.16	.6073	
Lower	547	2.46	.7017	
Functional Area				6.57*
Production	216	2.34	.6478	
Marketing	27	2.28	.8297	
Finance & Accounting	36	2.04	.5353	
Personnel	24	2.01	.5262	
General Management	252	2.06	.6822	
R&D	198	2.34	.6642	
Engineering	196	2.41	.7030	
Other	214	2.26	.7177	
Education				1.50
High school	136	2.18	.5829	
2-year college	231	2.26	.6986	
Bachelor's degree	529	2.25	.6913	
Master's degree	208	2.35	.7487	
Other	57	2.21	.6819	
Total Sample	1,163	2.26	.6915	

*$p < .05$.

organization or one or more of its subsystems are experiencing too little, too much, or a moderate amount of intrapersonal conflict. The normative data should be used with caution because they provide some crude indicators of what may be the normal level of conflict in an organization.

Sources

The sources of intrapersonal conflict are mainly structural; they are situationally imposed. The diagnosis of intrapersonal conflict must identify these sources so that they can be altered to attain and maintain a moderate amount of conflict.

Misassignment and Goal Incongruence. If a person is assigned to do a task for which he does not have the appropriate expertise, aptitude, and commitment, then the person may experience undesirable frustration. There are notable examples of misassignment in the military organization. Argyris' (1964, 1974) research on personality and organization theory shows that the needs of the individual and the goals of the organization are generally antithetical.

Argyris' (1974, p. 7) research shows that only top management felt absence of conflict between their own needs and the goals of the organization. The possibility suggests that there is an inverse relationship between organizational level and the perception of intrapersonal conflict. At the higher organizational level the employees have greater freedom to do the things they want to do to satisfy their individual needs as well as those of the organization. Unfortunately, there is no study which specifically investigated the relationship between organizational level and conflict.

Inappropriate Demand on Capacity. If a person cannot properly satisfy all the demands of his position even by working at the maximum capacity, then the demands overload the situation. If a person's capacity (skill, commitment, role expectation) significantly exceeds the demands of the position, then the person will not find his work challenging. A person may find his job challenging and motivating when the role demand slightly exceeds the individual's role expectation. Inadequate role demand is a common problem for young graduates who often find their jobs not as challenging as the academicians painted them to be.

Organization Structure. The structure of an organization has a major influence on role conflict (Kahn et al., 1964). Organizations generate a high degree of role conflict by creating conflicting goals and policies and decisions. A number of earlier studies found multiple lines of authority to be associated with role conflict and loss of organizational effectiveness (Evan, 1962; Kaplan, 1959; La Porte, 1965).

Low role conflict was associated with organizational practices which promote "personal development, formalization, adequacy of communication, planning, horizontal communication, top management receptiveness to ideas, coordination of work flow, adaptability to change and adequacy of authority" (Rizzo, House, & Lirtzman, 1970, p. 161). House and Rizzo (1972) found that organizational practices, such as formalization, planning activity, provision for horizontal coordination, selection based on ability, and adherence to chain of command are all negatively related to role conflict and ambiguity. Morris, Steers, and Koch (1979) concluded that employees may be allowed greater participation in decision making affecting their jobs to reduce role conflict and ambiguity.

Supervisory Style. This may be one of the major generators of role conflict. Rizzo et al. (1970) found role conflict to be lower when "supervisors are described as more frequently engaging in emphasizing production under conditions of uncertainty, providing structure and standards, facilitating teamwork, tolerating freedom, and exerting upward influence" (p. 161). House and Rizzo (1972) found negative relationship between role conflict and leader initiating structure and standard setting, which is directed at formalization, and supervisory supportiveness and team orientation.

Position. A classic position that is exposed to more role conflict than others is that of the foreman (Charters, 1952; Roethlisberger, 1965; Rosen, 1970). A foreman is often caught in the middle between the inconsistent demands from the supervisors and subordinates. Another classic position in an organization which is exposed to more role conflict is the salesman. Kahn et al. (1964) found that organization members, who were required to engage in boundary-spanning activities, i.e., make frequent outside contacts, experienced more role conflict. The studies by Organ and Greene (1974), Rogers and Molnar (1976), and Miles and Perreault (1976) provide further support to this relationship. Kahn et al. found a slight difference in the degree of role conflict reported by intra- and inter-organizational boundary spanners.

This section provided an approach to a comprehensive diagnosis. This should not be taken to mean that every organization needs or can afford such a diagnosis. The results of diagnosis should indicate whether there is any need for intervention and the type of intervention required. It should, at the minimum, indicate whether there is too much of this conflict and whether its effects are functional or dysfunctional. If it is felt that the effects of intrapersonal conflict on individual effectiveness are negligible or nonsignificant, there is no need for an intervention in such conflict. If the effects of intrapersonal conflict on individual effectiveness are found to be significantly negative, an intervention may be needed to reduce this conflict to enhance effectiveness.

Intervention

As discussed in Chapter 3, two types of intervention, behavioral and structural, are available for the management of conflict. These have been presented here for the management of intrapersonal conflict.

Behavioral

The technique of role analysis has been presented in this chapter as a behavioral intervention for managing intrapersonal conflict. Although this technique has been classified as a behavioral intervention, it contains the components of both behavioral and structural interventions.

Technique of Role Analysis. This method of intervention was first applied by Dayal and Thomas (1968) to help a new organization in India grow and increase its effectiveness. Role analysis is an intervention designed to improve overall organizational effectiveness by intervening at individual, group, and intergroup levels.

Application of this technique involves five distinct steps. A model of role analysis is utilized which involves examination of the purpose of the role, its prescribed and discretionary elements, and its relationship with other roles. The role analysis should ideally start with the top manager of the system being changed. The formal steps of the technique are as follows:

1. *Purpose of role.* The focal role occupant, i.e., individual whose role is being analyzed, initiates the discussion relating to his role. The group members or their representatives discuss the purpose of the role, i.e., how the role fits in with the goals of the organization and/or subsystems.

2. *Role perception.* The focal role occupant lists the activities she or he feels occupy his role. Participants discuss the items, ask for explanations and, as a result, new items are added and ambiguous or contradictory items are dropped. The participants help the role incumbent to analyze the prescribed and discretionary components of the role. This frequently "enables the individual to clarify the responsibility he must take on himself for decisions, the choices open to him for alternative courses of action, and new competencies he must develop in his assigned role" (Dayal & Thomas, 1968, p. 487).

3. *Expectations of role occupant.* The focal role occupant lists his expectations from his group members. Members of the group discuss these expectations to clarify role interdependencies; a mutually acceptable solution is reached describing expectations and obligations.

4. *Expectations from role occupant.* Each participant presents his list of expectations from the focal role which represents the group's views of the participant's obligation to the group member in performing his role. Here much of the process in step 3 is repeated for each participant.

5. *Role profile.* The focal role occupant is made responsible for writing down the main points of the discussion called a role profile. This consists of (a) prescribed and discretionary activities, (b) obligation of this role to other roles in the group, and (c) expectations of someone in his role to other roles in the group.

This technique can be used to analyze and differentiate individual, group, and intergroup roles and to help the individuals in managing tasks and role interdependencies more systematically. The latter is attained through the analysis of role relationships and reassignment of tasks which provide a better match between the needs of the individual and the task goals. From the foregoing analysis, it appears that role analysis may not only affect conflict at the individual level but also at the group and intergroup levels.

Structural

This section presents job design as a structural intervention for managing intrapersonal conflict.

Job Design. It involves the planning of the job, including its contents, the methods of performing the job, and how it relates to other jobs in the organization. Job design method can follow two approaches. The classical approach involves structuring the task activities to make full use of the division of labor and specialization. This job engineering is still a popular job design strategy. The second approach involves changing the job to make it satisfying. This is called job enrichment.

Herzberg's two-factor theory provided real impetus to job enrichment (Herzberg, Mausner, & Snyderman, 1959). Herzberg's approach to job enrichment involves improvement of the motivation factors, such as achievement, recognition, responsibility, advancement, and opportunity for growth. This approach is based on the assumption that job enrichment increases job satisfaction, which in turn increases motivation and better performance. Herzberg et al. (1959) suggested that improvement in the hygiene factors, such as salary, company policies, working conditions, etc., do not lead to increase in employee motivation. The theory has been criticized on the grounds of (a) failure to provide the evidence of existence of two factors, such as motivation and hygiene, (b) assuming that motivating factors increase motivation of all employees, and (c) failure to specify how motivating factors can be measured for existing jobs (Hackman & Oldham, 1976).

Another approach to job enrichment, recently developed by Hackman and Oldham (1980), is shown in Figure 4.2. Their approach attempts to make jobs more meaningful by increasing or adding certain core job characteristics, such as skill variety, task identity, task significance, autonomy, and feedback. This approach attempts to remedy some of the problems in Herzberg et al.'s approach.

Building on the works of Turner and Lawrence (1965), Hackman and Oldham (1975) identified five core dimensions that must be considered in enriching a job. These dimensions are positively related to motivation, satisfaction, and quality of work, and negatively related to turnover and absenteeism. It is expected that these five dimensions will negatively relate to intrapersonal conflict. The five core dimensions can be described as follows (Hackman & Oldham, 1975):

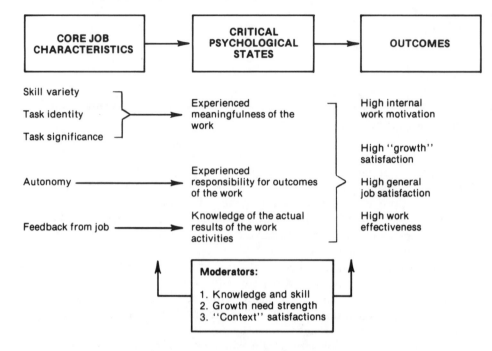

FIGURE 4.2. The Job Characteristics Model

1. *Skill variety*. This is the degree to which a job requires a variety of activities which involve the use of a number of different skills and talents of the employee.
2. *Task identity*. This is the degree to which the job requires an employee to perform a complete piece of work, i.e., doing a job from beginning to end with a visible outcome.
3. *Task significance*. It refers to the degree to which the job has an impact on the lives or work of other people, within or outside the organization.
4. *Autonomy*. This is the degree to which the job provides freedom, independence, and discretion to the employee in scheduling his or her work and in determining the procedures to be used in carrying it out.
5. *Feedback*. This refers to the amount of information which results from the performance of a job by an employee about how well he or she is performing.

As shown in Figure 4.2, the core dimensions influence three critical psychological states. The jobs which are high on skill variety, task identifying, and task significance influence experienced meaningfulness of the work. Psychological states, such as experienced responsibility for outcomes of the work, and knowledge of the actual results of the work activities are influenced by job autonomy and feedback, respectively. Accoriding to this theory, higher level of psychological states lead to positive personal and work outcomes, such as high internal work motivation, high growth satisfaction, high general job satisfaction, and high work effectiveness.

Hackman and Oldham devised the following equation for computing an overall index, the Motivation Potential Score (MPS):

$$\text{MSP} = \frac{(\text{Skill Variety} + \text{Task Identity} + \text{Task Significance})}{3}$$

$$\times \text{Autonomy} \times \text{Feedback}$$

The MPS was hypothesized to be positively related to personal and work outcomes, but because individual employees differ, the researchers suggested that every employee does not respond to the MPS identically. There are three factors which moderate the relationship between the core job characteristics and outcomes. These are:

1. Knowledge and skill of the employees to perform job well.
2. Growth need strength, i.e., need for learning, self-direction, and personal growth of the employees.
3. "Context" satisfactions, i.e., the level of satisfaction particularly with job security, compensation, co-workers, and supervision.

The employees who report higher on one or more of the above moderators should respond more postively to jobs which score high on MPS. "The 'worst possible' circumstance for a job that is high in motivating potential, for example, would be when the job incumbent is only marginally competent to perform the work *and* has low needs for personal growth at work *and* is highly dissatisfied with one or more aspects of the work context. The job clearly would be too much for that individual, and negative personal and work outcomes would be predicted" (Hackman & Oldham, 1980, p. 88).

The researchers designed an instrument, called Job Diagnostic Survey, for measuring each of the variables in the job characteristics model (Hackman & Oldham, 1975). In a recent study, Hackman and Oldham (1976) found moderate support for their theory.

In a study of seventy-seven nursing aids and assistants in a large university hospital, Brief and Aldag (1976) found negative relations between role conflict and the perceptions of five core task dimensions. But only the relations between role conflict and task identity and autonomy were statistically significant.

The Job Characteristics Model appears to be a useful conceptual framework for studying the effects of job design on work behavior and performance of individual employees. The model is in its early stage of development; therefore, further studies are necessary to investigate the effects of job design on conflict.

SUMMARY

Kurt Lewin (1948) defined conflict as a situation in which opposing and simultaneously occurring forces of about equal strength occur in a person. The three types of this conflict are approach-approach conflict, approach-avoidance conflict, and avoidance-avoidance conflict. Perceived incompatibilities or incongruencies frequently occur when an organizational participant is required to perform a role or task which does not match his expertise, interests, goals, and values.

Role conflict occurs when the focal perosn is expected to perform incompatible or inconsistent role expectations communicated by his role senders. Kahn et al. identified four types of role conflict, such as intrasender, intersender, interrole, and intrarole conflicts. Role overload is a form of intersender conflict. Kahn et al. presented role conflict through a series of events or a role episode. A concept related to role conflict is role ambiguity, which refers to the lack of understanding of what expectations or prescriptions exist for a given role. The consequences of role conflict include job dissatisfaction, tension and anxiety, propensity to leave, lack of confidence in the organization, and inability to influence in decision making.

The management of intrapersonal conflict involves diagnosis and intervention. The diagnosis should essentially indicate whether there is too much of intrapersonal conflict in an organization and whether its effects on individual effectiveness are dysfunctional. The sources of intrapersonal conflict are misassignment and goal incongruence, inappropriate demand on capacity, organization structure, supervisory style, and position. These sources may be altered to reduce or generate conflict. Intervention is needed when the effect of intrapersonal conflict on organizational participants becomes dysfunctional. Two major intervention techniques, such as role analysis and job design, are available for the management of intrapersonal conflict.

REFERENCES

Argyris, C. (1964). *Integrating the individual and the organization*. New York: Wiley.

Argyris, C. (1974). Personality vs. organization. *Organizational Dynamics, 3*(2), 3–17.

Brief, A. P., & Aldag, R. J. (1976). Correlates of role indices. *Journal of Applied Psychology, 61*, 468–472.

Charters, W. W. (1952). A study of role conflict among foremen in a heavy industry. Unpublished doctoral dissertation, University of Michigan.

Conway, M. M., & Feigert, F. B. (1976). *Political analysis: An introduction* (2nd *Ed.*). Boston: Allyn and Bacon.

Dayal, I., & Thomas, J. M. (1968). Operation KPE: Developing a new organization. *Journal of Applied Behavioral Science, 4*, 473–506.

Evan, W. M. (1962). Role strain and the norm of reciprocity in research organizations. *American Journal of Sociology, 68*, 346–354.

Getzels, J. W., & Guba, E. G. (1954). Role, role conflict and effectiveness: An empirical study. *American Sociological Review, 19*, 164–175.

Greene, C. N., & Organ, D. W. (1973). An evaluation of causal models linking the perceived role with job satisfaction. *Administrative Science Quarterly, 18*, 95–103.

Hackman, J. R., & Oldham, G. R. (1975). Development of the job diagnostic survey. *Journal of Applied Psychology, 60*, 159–170.

Hackman, J. R., & Oldham, G. R. (1976). Motivation through the design of work: Test of a theory. *Organizational Behavior and Human Performance, 16*, 250–279.

Hackman, J. R., & Oldham, G. R. (1980). *Work redesign*. Reading, MA.: Addison-Wesley.

Hamner, W. C., & Tosi, H. L. (1974). Relationship of role conflict and role ambiguity to job involvement measures. *Journal of Applied Psychology, 59*, 497–499.

Herzberg, F., Mausner, B., & Snyderman, B. (1959). *The motivation to work*. New York: Wiley.

House, R. J., & Rizzo, J. R. (1972). Role conflict and ambiguity as critical variables in a model of organizational behavior. *Organizational Behavior and Human Performance, 7*, 467–505.

Ivancevich, J. M., & Donnelly, J. H., Jr. (1974). A study of role clarity and need for clarity for three occupational groups. *Academy of Management Journal, 17*, 28–36.

Johnson, T. W., & Stinson, J. E. (1975). Role ambiguity, role conflict, and satisfaction: Moderating effects of individual differences. *Journal of Applied Psychology, 60*, 329–333.

Kahn, R. L., Wolfe, D. M., Quinn, P. R., Snoak, J. D., & Rosenthal, R. A. (1964). *Organization stress: Studies in role conflict and ambiguity*. New York: Wiley.

Kaplan, N. (1959). The role of the research administrator. *Administrative Science Quarterly, 4*, 20–42.

LaPorte, R. T. (1965). Conditions of strain and accommodation in industrial research organizations. *Administrative Science Quarterly, 10,* 21–38.

Lewin, K. (1948). *Resolving social conflicts: Selected papers on group dynamics* (Ed. by G. W. Lewin). New York: Harper.

Lyons, T. F. (1971). Role clarity, need for clarity, satisfaction, tension, and withdrawal. *Organizational Behavior and Human Performance, 6,* 99–110.

Miles, R. H. (1975). An empirical test of causal inference between role perceptions of conflict and ambiguity and various personal outcomes. *Journal of Applied Psychology, 60,* 334–339.

Miles, R. H., & Perreault, W. D., Jr. (1976). Organizational role conflict: Its antecedents and consequences. *Organizational Behavior and Human Performance, 17,* 19–44.

Morris, J. H., Steers, R. M., & Koch, J. L. (1979). Influence of organization structure on role conflict and ambiguity for three occupational groupings. *Academy of Management Journal, 22,* 58–71.

Murray, E. J. (1968). Conflict: I. Psychological aspects. In D. L. Sills (Ed.), *International encyclopedia of the social sciences* (Vol. 3, pp. 220–226). New York: Crowell and Macmillan.

Organ, D. W., & Greene, C. N. (1974). Role ambiguity, locus of control, and work satisfaction. *Journal of Applied Psychology, 59,* 101–102.

Rahim, M. A. (1983). Measurement of organizational conflict. *Journal of General Psychology, 109,* 189–199.

Rizzo, J. R., House, R. J., & Lirtzman, S. I. (1970). Role conflict and ambiguity in complex organizations. *Administrative Science Quarterly, 15,* 150–163.

Roethlisberger, F. J. (1965). The foreman: Master and victim of double talk. *Harvard Business Review, 43* (5), 22–26ff.

Rogers, D. L., & Molnar, J. (1976). Organizational antecedents of role conflict and ambiguity in top level administrators. *Administrative Science Quarterly, 21,* 598–610.

Rosen, R. A. H. (1970). Foreman role conflict: An expression of contradictions in organizational goals. *Industrial and Labor Relations Review, 23,* 541–552.

Sales, S. M. (1969). Organizational role as a risk factor in coronary disease. *Administrative Science Quarterly, 14,* 325–336.

Sarbin, T. R. (1968). Role: Psychological aspects. In D. L. Sills (Ed.), *International encyclopedia of the social sciences* (Vol. 13 pp. 546–552). New York: Macmillan and Free Press.

Tosi, H. (1971). Organization stress as a moderator of the relationship between influence and role response. *Academy of Management Journal, 14,* 7–20.

Turner, A. N., & Lawrence, P. R. (1965). *Industrial jobs and the worker: An investigation of response to task attitudes.* Cambridge, MA.: Harvard University Press.

5

Interpersonal Conflict

Interpersonal conflict involves incompatibility, disagreement, or difference between two or more persons. As discussed in Chapters 2 and 3, there are several styles of handling interpersonal conflict, such as integrating, obliging, dominating, avoiding, and compromising. This chapter discusses the styles of handling conflict of an organizational member with his superior(s), subordinates, and peers. This is because most of the literature on interpersonal conflict in organizations deals with the styles of handling interpersonal conflict rather than the amount of such conflict. A number of studies on interpersonal conflict deal mainly with superior-subordinate conflict.

A MODEL OF CONFLICT

Over the years a number of models have been developed to illustrate the dynamics of different types of organizational conflict. Instead of developing a separate model for each type of organizational conflict, an integrated model has been developed which can be used to illustrate the dynamics of interpersonal, intragroup, and intergroup conflicts.

There are various models which present organizational conflict as a process. Goldman (1966) presented a cycle of conflict based on: (a) an initiating event, (b) an influencing event, and (c) a concluding event. Pondy (1967) presented a model of organizational conflict which identified five stages of conflict episode: (a) latent conflict, (b) perceived conflict, (c) felt conflict, (d) manifest conflict, and (e) conflict aftermath. Walton and Dutton (1969) presented a model of interdepartmental conflict which focused on the (a) determinants of conflict, (b) attributes

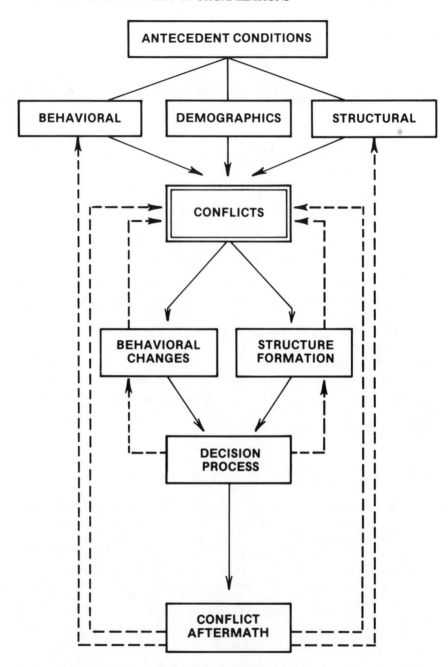

FIGURE 5.1. A Model of Organizational Conflict

or manifestations of conflict, and (c) consequences of the relationship patterns of organizational effectiveness. Thomas' (1976) process model of conflict episode includes frustration, conceptualization, behavior, and outcome.

Figure 5.1 presents a theoretical model of organizational conflict, especially interpersonal, intragroup, and intergroup conflicts. This model is based on the voluminous literature on the subject, especially the ones reviewed above. The model can be used in formulating and testing hypotheses and thereby validating the model itself. Hopefully this model will enable an organizational interventionist to manage conflict effectively.

Antecedent Conditions. The model begins with the antecedent conditions or sources of conflict. The sources of conflict can be classified as behavioral and structural. Extensive treatments of these two sources of conflict have been provided in this and the following two chapters. The model also shows that demographic factors, such as sex, age, tenure, education, etc., may also affect conflict (Rahim, 1980).

Behavioral Changes. Conflict may affect the behavior and attitudes of parties toward each other. If the conflict becomes intense, the parties move away from a congenial and trusting relationship and redirect their energies toward the goal of winning. Since the immediate goal of each party is to win or control the situation, the interest in the solution of the problem(s) becomes less important. In other words, the parties may become less prepared to contribute to organizational goals effectively.

One of the possible consequences of intense conflict is the distortion in the perception of the parties. The perceptual distortion may become progressively greater and each party may consider the other party an enemy and they may describe each other with negative stereotypes. As a result, it will be more difficult for the parties to gather and evaluate information objectively to resolve their conflict constructively.

The parties may attempt to make greater use of the win-lose method to deal with their conflict. If both parties are equally powerful, they may use dominating style to handle their differences and disagreements. If they fail to reach an agreement, they may change their style from dominating to compromising to resolve the conflict. If there are differences in power between the parties (e.g., superior and subordinate), the more powerful party may impose a solution on the less powerful party, i.e., use a dominating style. The less powerful party may be forced to use an avoiding style, i.e., accept the decision given by the more powerful party without protest, to deal with the situation.

Structure Formation. As the conflict intensifies, the parties may restrict free communication and interaction. The parties may decide to communicate with each other only through writing. In other words, the parties may formulate a structure of interaction which discourages free exchange of information. All contacts between the parties become formal, rigid, and carefully defined. In a bureaucratic organization, the parties may take the help of rules and regulations that may exist to deal with the situation(s). In some situations, a party may come up with different interpretations of a rule so that a decision can be made in her or his favor.

Decision Process. When win-lose conflict is intensified, the parties may be unable to use problem-solving methods to make decisions to resolve their differences. Instead they may establish a medium of negotiation which is generally bargaining. When two large powerful social entities are involved, the bargaining sessions may be extremely formal and lengthy. If the conflicting groups fail to reach a decision, an arbitrator may be selected by the parties to break the deadlock.

In the case of conflict within a group, decision is often made by majority vote. This process of decision making may lead to a split between two or more subgroups within a group.

In the case of superior-subordinate conflict, the decision is often made by the superior and communicated to the subordinate. In many cases the organizations allow subordinates to go to a higher level executive to discuss their grievances. Many organizations allow the lower level employees to take their problems to grievance committees.

In the case of conflict between two managers at the same organizational level, the superior of the two parties is often called upon to make a decision to "resolve" the conflict. The same decision process may be used when two departments or units fail to resolve their conflicts in a reasonable manner.

Conflict Aftermath. "Usually the resolution of conflict leaves a legacy which will affect the future relations of the parties and their attitudes toward each other" (Filley, 1975, p. 17). If bargaining and compromising are exclusively utilized as a method of conflict resolution, there is a possibility that both parties will perceive themselves as partly losers after the cessation of conflict. If one party is clearly a loser after a resolution, this party may have antagonistic feelings toward the other party which may affect the generation and resolution of another conflict. The resolution of a win-lose conflict may not only affect the behavior and attitudes of the parties for each other, it may also affect organization structure. The conflicting parties or their superior may formulate more rules and procedures, or clarify the existing ones, to deal with future conflict between the parties.

If the parties use problem-solving or integrating style to deal with their conflict, this may reduce the psychological distance between them. They may be more prepared to deal with their disagreements in a more constructive manner which involves exchange of information and open communication. A problem-solving approach for the management of conflict may lead to greater commitment to the agreement reached between parties.

CONSEQUENCES OF INTERPERSONAL CONFLICT

One would expect the outcomes of interpersonal conflict that fully satisfy the outcomes of both parties to be functional for an organization. Previous studies generally indicate that problem-solving or integrating style by the members of an organization leads to greater satisfaction of the organizational members. However, there is no evidence to suggest that greater use of integrating style of handling conflict leads to greater organizational effectiveness.

A study by Aram, Morgan, and Esbeck (1971) suggested that team collaboration was positively related to satisfaction of individuals' needs, but not to organizational performance. Burke (1970) suggested that, in general, confrontation (integrating) style was related to effective conflict resolution and forcing (dominating) and withdrawing (avoiding) were related to ineffective resolution of conflict. Lawrence and Lorsch (1967) indicated that confrontation style to deal with intergroup conflict was used to a significantly greater degree in higher than lower performing organizations. Likert and Likert (1976) strongly argued and provided some evidence to suggest that an organization which encourages participation and problem-solving behaviors attains a higher level of effectiveness.

As discussed in Chapter 3, all the five styles of handling conflict are useful depending on situations. For example, an integrating style is not appropriate unless the issues involved in a conflict are complex or strategic. The situations where each style is appropriate or inappropriate were presented in Table 3.1.

MANAGING INTERPERSONAL CONFLICT

The management of interpersonal conflict involves changes in the attitudes, behavior, and organization structure, so that the organizational members can work with each other effectively for attaining their individual and/or joint goals. The management of interpersonal conflict essentially involves the training of organizational members to enable them to learn the styles of handling interpersonal conflict to deal with different situations effectively; and setting up appropriate mechanisms so that unresolved issues are dealt with properly. The management of interpersonal conflict, which involves diagnosis and intervention, is discussed as follows.

Diagnosis

The diagnosis of interpersonal conflict can be performed by such methods as self-reports, observation, and interiews. The Rahim Organizational Conflict Inventory-II(ROCI-II) may be used to measure how an organizational member handles his interpersonal conflict with superior(s) (Form A), subordinates (Form B), and peers (Form C). There are five other instruments for measuring the overall modes (styles) of handling interpersonal conflict. These instruments were designed by Blake and Mouton (1964), Hall (1969), Lawrence and Lorsch (1967), Putnam and Wilson (1982), and Thomas and Kilmann (1974). Thomas and Kilmann's (1978) study concluded that the reliability coefficients for the Blake and Mouton, Hall, Lawrence and Lorsch, and Thomas and Kilmann "instruments fall within low-to-moderate range" (p. 1142).

Rahim (1983) was able to design the ROCI-II containing five factorially independent scales for measuring the five styles of handling interpersonal conflict with superiors, subordinates, or peers. Factor analysis of the items of the Lawrence and Lorsch instrument resulted in three instead of five factors (Lawrence & Lorsch, 1967; see also Fry, Kidron, Osborn, & Tafton, 1980; Prein, 1976). Putnam and Wilson (1982) were also unable to obtain the five-factor solution for their Organizational Communication Conflict Instrument. They adopted a three-factor solution, such as nonconfrontation, solution-orientation, and control.

A comprehensive diagnosis of interpersonal conflict involves the *measurement* of the following:

1. The styles of handling interpersonal conflict used by the organizational members to deal with different situations.
2. Factors which affect the styles of handling conflict.
3. Effectiveness of the individual members of an organization.

An *analysis* of the above diagnostic data should provide the following information:

1. The styles of handling interpersonal conflict utilized by the members of various units, departments, or divisions, and whether they deviated from the national norms significantly.

2. Whether organizational members are using appropriate behavioral styles to deal with different situations effectively.
3. Relationships between the styles, situations, and individual effectiveness.

National Norms

Data for national norms of the styles of handling interpersonal conflict with superior(s), subordinates, and peers were derived from a study conducted to test the reliability and validity of the ROCI-II (Rahim, 1983). In this study, about an equal number of Forms A, B, and C were sent to 4,000 executives who were randomly selected from the Penton/IPC list of 1.3 million organizational members. These executives were from 25 different industries. A cover letter explaining the purpose of the study accompanied the inventory. Usable responses were received from 1,219 executives, a response rate of about 31 percent. Although the response rate was only moderately satisfactory, a follow-up letter was not sent because funds were limited. Tables 5.1 and 5.2 were prepared on the basis of this sample.

Table 5.1 shows the national percentile norms of managers. The percentile score of an individual shows his or her relative position on one of the five scales of the styles of handling interpersonal conflict with superior(s), subordinates, and peers compared with other managers in the normative group. For example, a manager scoring at the 70th percentile on a scale is as high or higher than 70 percent of the normative group. His or her score is exceeded by only 30 percent of the normative group.

Table 5.2 shows the sample size (N), means (M) (reference group norms), standard deviations (SD) of the five styles of handling interpersonal conflict, classified by referent role, organizational level, functional area, and education, and the results of one-way analyses of variance (F).

The results of the analyses of variance show that there were significant differences in each style of handling conflict with superior(s), subordinates, and peers. This suggests that the styles of handling conflict of an organizational member are, to some extent, determined by the hierarchial relationship that exists between the parties involved in conflict. There were also differences in obliging and avoiding styles among the executives across organizational levels, in obliging style across the functional area, and in dominating and avoiding styles across the educational categories.

The normative data are useful in determining whether the members

TABLE 5.1. Managerial Percentile Norms of Styles of Handling Interpersonal Conflict with Superior (Form A), Subordinates (Form B), and Peers (Form C) (N = 1,219)

									Percentiles								
Mean Score	Form A (n = 452)						Form B (n = 363)					Form C (n = 404)				Mean Score
	IN *	OB	DO	AV	CO	IN	OB	DO	AV	CO	IN	OB	DO	AV	CO	
5.00	99					99					99					5.00
4.85	95		99			95					95					4.85
4.70	90	99	98		99	90					87				99	4.70
4.55	84	97	97	99	98	79					81		99		98	4.55
4.40	76	96	96	98	95	69				99	74	99	98	99	96	4.40
4.25	66	92	95	96	94	59	99	99	99	98	62	98	97	98	94	4.25
4.10	51	88	94	94	92	44	98	98	98	97	50	97	96	97	91	4.10
3.95	35	79	90	91	85	28	97	96	97	92	30	95	92	96	83	3.95
3.80	13	61	82	88	68	7	94	92	93	80	11	92	86	92	62	3.80
3.65	10	58	67	85	58	5	88	88	91	62	6	86	81	91	50	3.65
3.50	6	45	60	78	51	3	77	82	88	61	3	76	66	88	42	3.50
3.35	4	35	53	74	35	2	65	75	80	45	1	63	64	84	34	3.35

3.20	3	24	51	68	34	1	52	71	76	41	51	58	76	28	3.20
3.05	2	17	41	63	27		41	61	70	37	41	49	74	23	3.05
2.90	1	10	33	57	21		29	52	62	32	29	41	67	19	2.90
2.75		7	27	51	15		17	36	54	26	20	24	57	14	2.75
2.60		5	20	45	12		14	35	47	22	14	23	44	10	2.60
2.45		3	17	35	11		9	30	38	17	9	18	42	9	2.45
2.30		2	12	28	6		5	23	31	10	6	13	35	7	2.30
2.15		1	8	20	5		4	16	22	9	3	9	24	6	2.15
2.00			7	16	4		2	11	16	7	2	6	19	5	2.00
1.85			3	11	2		1	6	9	4	1	3	11	3	1.85
1.70			2	8	1			4	6	2		2	8	1	1.70
1.55			1	4				3	4	1		1	5		1.55
1.40				2				2	3				3		1.40
1.25				1				1	1				2		1.25
1.10													1		1.10
1.00															1.00

*IN = Integrating, OB = Obliging, DO = Dominating, AV = Avoiding, CO = Compromising.

TABLE 5.2 Managerial Reference Group Norms of Styles of Handling Interpersonal Conflict with Superior (Form A), Subordinates (Form B), and Peers (Form C) ($N = 1,219$)

Variables	N	Integrating			Obliging		
		M	SD	F	M	SD	F
Role Status				4.66*			77.47*
Superior	451	4.18	.4328		3.60	.5337	
Subordinates	363	4.26	.3939		3.21	.4908	
Peers	404	4.24	.3835		3.24	.5120	
Organizational Level				0.46			8.29*
Top	176	4.24	.4946		3.22	.5897	
Middle	501	4.23	.3974		3.36	.5289	
Lower	515	4.21	.3824		3.41	.5311	
Functional Area				1.81			2.22*
Production	253	4.16	.3896		3.37	.5403	
Marketing	32	4.22	.3892		3.39	.5298	
Finance & Accounting	28	4.24	.4434		3.34	.5452	
Personnel	35	4.30	.3580		3.48	.4717	
General Management	287	4.27	.4478		3.27	.5736	
R&D	200	4.22	.3935		3.45	.5481	
Engineering	181	4.24	.3910		3.38	.5145	
Other	197	4.22	.3786		3.37	.5361	
Education				0.93			1.36
High school	145	4.19	.3581		3.37	.4940	
2-year college	233	4.21	.4186		3.32	.5322	
Bachelor's degree	572	4.25	.3895		3.40	.5429	
Master's degree	202	4.21	.4418		3.32	.5567	
Other	64	4.20	.4979		3.38	.6640	
Total Sample	1,218	4.22	.4067		3.36	.5454	

*$p < .05$

of an organization are making too little, too much, or moderate use of each style of handling interpersonal conflict. But normative data cannot indicate whether the styles are properly used to deal with different situations.

Sources

As will be evident in later chapters, a number of studies have investigated the sources of intraorganizational conflict in general. However, the factors which affect the styles of handling conflict have not been adequately investigated. Several factors, such as personality, bases

Dominating			Avoiding			Compromising		
M	*SD*	*F*	*M*	*SD*	*F*	*M*	*SD*	*F*
		24.19*			5.63*			17.44*
3.27	.6849		2.89	.7834		3.51	.6379	
2.94	.6655		2.78	.6789		3.31	.6929	
3.16	.6560		2.72	.7134		3.59	.6584	
		1.69			3.63*			1.32
3.21	.7020		2.67	.7533		3.43	.6833	
3.15	.6690		2.80	.7397		3.46	.6826	
3.10	.6863		2.84	.7122		3.51	.6536	
		1.36			1.44			0.75
3.08	.6759		2.84	.7344		3.46	.6624	
3.26	.5912		2.69	.6670		3.59	.6301	
2.94	.6752		2.79	.7894		3.32	.6910	
3.23	.5708		2.67	.6420		3.59	.6270	
3.17	.7049		2.70	.7563		3.50	.6686	
3.16	.6598		2.81	.7165		3.52	.6816	
3.06	.6281		2.84	.6937		3.44	.6334	
3.17	.7542		2.87	.7642		3.45	.7149	
		5.75*			5.41*			0.57
3.01	.7204		2.97	.6711		3.50	.6502	
3.03	.6405		2.91	.7604		3.44	.6797	
3.15	.6837		2.76	.7092		3.50	.6633	
3.30	.6468		2.67	.7581		3.44	.6889	
3.14	.7436		2.77	.7983		3.45	.6975	
3.13	.6823		2.80	.7331		3.48	.6703	

of power, organizational climate, and referent role affect not only interpersonal but also intragroup and intergroup conflicts. Instead of discussing their effects on different types of conflict in separate chapters, their effects have been presented in an integrated fashion in this chapter.

Personality. After a thorough review of the experimental studies on personality and conflict, Terhune (1970) concluded that "personality effects do seem influential and highly important in cooperation-conflict behavior ... certainly the researcher should not be discouraged if personality effects do not just 'pop out' on first analysis, especially in complex situations" (p. 230).

Kilmann and Thomas (1975) explored the relations between the five modes (styles) of handling interpersonal conflict and the four dimensions of Jungian (Jung, 1923) personality, such as sensing-intuition, thinking-feeling, introvert-extravert, and judging-perceiving, as measured by Myers-Briggs Type Indicator (Myers, 1962). The results showed that the extraverts are more likely to strive for collaborative or integrative style of handling conflict than introverts. This and other field studies (e.g., Bell & Blakeney, 1977; Jones & Melcher, 1982) found low correlations between personality and the styles of handling interpersonal conflict. This may be partly attributed to the failure of the researchers to control the hierarchial relationship between the parties involved in conflict and the situations or issues involved in conflict.

Review of experimental studies by Walton and McKersie (1965) found that certain personality attributes, such as authoritarianism and dogmatism, are positively related to conflict. They found self-esteem inversely related to conflict behavior.

Bases of Power. A number of studies have been conducted to demonstrate the effects of French and Raven's (1959) bases of power (coercive, reward, expert, legitimate, and referent) of the superior on the work performance and satisfaction of the subordinates. However, the organization theorists neglected to examine the effects of a superior's bases of power on interpersonal conflict and the selection and use of the styles of handling such conflict by subordinates.

Raven and Kruglanski (1970) reviewed numerous studies to examine the relationship between social power and social conflict and concluded that the "power analysis provided a richer basis for the analysis of dyadic conflict" (p. 105). They also concluded that the analysis becomes complex when it is applied to other types of conflicts. Stern and Gorman (1969) suggested, in connection with intrachannel conflict, that "the exercise of power is a major conflict response as well as a cause of conflict" (p. 161). In a study of automobile manufacturers and their dealer network, Lusch (1976) indicated that coercive sources of power increased, and non-coercive sources of power (reward, expert, legitimate, and referent) decreased manufacturer-dealer conflict.

Jamieson and Thomas (1974) examined students' perception of their teachers' bases of power and their own modes of handling conflict with teachers. The students (at the high school and undergraduate levels) reported somewhat less accommodating (obliging) and somewhat more competing (dominating) with teachers who used more coercive power. Coercive power was positively correlated with competing (dominating) mode at the graduate level. Referent power induced accommodating (obliging) mode at the high school and undergraduate level and collaborating (integrating) modes at the graduate level.

Organizational Climate. Likert and Likert (1976) persuasively argued and provided some evidence that a more positive climate, such as System IV, can provide for a more functional management of conflict than Systems I, II, or III. Likert (1967) classified his Systems I, II, III, and IV as exploitive-authoritative, benevolent-authoritative, consultative, and participative organizations, respectively. It is expected that a more positive climate will enable the members to confront their disagreements and disputes in a constructive fashion so that problems are identified and corrective measures taken. As a result, dysfunctional conflicts experienced by the organization members are reduced.

Referent Role. Organizations plant the seeds of conflict by allowing different statuses to different people. In superior-suoordinate communication, subordinates frequently say what is acceptable rather than what they know it true. This is especially true when superiors are authoritarian and regard their subordinates as inferiors. Therefore, it is natural to assume that an individual would probably make more of an effort to use obliging style with a superior than with a subordinate or peer.

Since subordinates are likely to withdraw from a conflict situation (Kahn, Wolfe, Quinn, Snoak, & Rosenthal, 1964) it would be expected that individuals would be more likely to use the avoiding style with superiors than with peers and more with peers than subordinates. A study by Phillips and Cheston (1979) reported that a forcing (dominating) approach is the most common in handling differences with subordinates than with peers and much less with superiors. Compromising approach is the most common to those conflict situations in which both parties have equal power (peers). Therefore, it would be expected that compromising style would be more likely to be used as a means of resolving conflict in dealing with peers than in dealing with either superiors or subordinates. A study by Rahim (1983) shows how managers handle their interpersonal conflict with superiors, subordinates, and peers. The executives are more obliging with their bosses and integrating and compromising with their subordinates and peers.

Musser (1982) presented a decisional model to show how a subordinate actually chooses a behavioral style to deal with high-stakes conflict with superior(s). A subordinate selects one of the five styles of handling conflict (strategies) depending on his or her response to each of the variables, such as subordinate's desire to remain in the organization, subordinate's perceived congruence between the superior's and his or her own attitudes and beliefs, and the subordinate's perceived protection from arbitrary action.

A study by Renwick (1975) attempted to determine if organizational status (superior-subordinate) influenced the conflict-handling modes likely to be adopted. Her findings were that organizational status did not affect the likelihood with which each of the five modes of conflict resolution would be used. This discrepency may possibly be attributed to the single-item instrument she used to measure the five conflict modes. Kilmann and Thomas (1977) found average test-retest reliability of the Blake and Mouton single-item instrument to be the lowest ($r = .39$) of the existing instruments on conflict modes.

Sex. Rahim (1983) investigated the differences in the styles of handling interpersonal conflict of men and women and found women to be more integrating, avoiding, and compromising and less obliging than men. These findings are consistent with the results reported by Kilmann and Thomas (1977). However, Renwick (1977) reported that "no differences were observed between the likelihood with which male and female subordinates would use various methods to deal with disagreements" (p. 403). As mentioned above, the findings of her study were probably influenced by the type of instrument she used to measure the conflict modes.

A diagnosis should particularly indicate whether the organizational participants are relying too much on one or more behavioral styles (e.g., dominating or avoiding) to deal with interpersonal conflict. A diagnosis should also indicate whether the organizational members are selecting and using appropriate behavioral styles to deal with different situations. Intervention is necessary when the organizational members have difficulty in dealing with different situations with appropriate behavioral styles.

Intervention

The behavioral and structural intervention strategies for the management of interpersonal conflict are presented as follows.

Behavioral

The objective of a behavioral intervention is to help the organizational members to enhance their integrating style of handling conflict by changing their attitudes and behavior. If the diagnosis indicates that the members of an organization or one or more of its subsystems are having difficulty in the selection and use of integrating style and/or they are making frequent use of other styles, a transactional analysis training may be useful for them.

Transactional Analysis. Developed by Berne (1961, 1964) and provided a clear and popular presentation by Harris (1969), and James and Jongeward (1971), transactional analysis provides better understanding of social transactions which involve interactions between two individuals. A transactional analysis intervention can enable the members of an organization to improve their communication and consequently the styles of handling conflict with superiors, subordinates, and peers.

The three aspects of transactional analysis are structural analysis, transactional analysis proper, and life positions. The following is a discussion of these three aspects.

1. *Structural, or personality, analysis* is the study of *ego states*. Human beings interact with each other in terms of three psychological states: Parent (P), Adult (A), and Child (C). The three ego states exist in each individual. Berne (1972) defined ego states as "coherent systems of thought and feeling manifested by corresponding patterns of behavior" (p. 11). The three ego states can be described as follows:

(a) *Parent ego state* reflects the attitudes, values, and behavior of authority figures, especially parents. This state may include prejudicial, critical, manipulative, or nurturing attitudes and behavior.

(b) *Adult ego state* represents the rational part of personality. It is based upon reason, collecting and processing information for problem solving, and discussion on the basis of evidence and information. It assumes that human beings are equal, important, and reasonable.

(c) *Child ego state* reflects the experiences and conditions of early childhood. In this state, the individual thinks, feels, and behaves just the way she or he did as a child.

The next section discusses how these ego states affect the interactions among individuals.

2. *Transactional analysis proper*. The three ego states are present in every individual and they affect the interactions of a person with others. When a person A communicates with person B, person A is in a distinct ego state and can direct her or his message to any of the three ego states of person B. The basic unit of communication is called a transaction. Transactions may be classified as complementary, crossed, or ulterior.

(a) *Complementary transaction* occurs when they are parallel, i.e., a message sent from one ego state (e.g., Parent) receives an expected response from the appropriate ego state of the other party (e.g., Child). In other words, *"when stimulus and response on the P-A-C transaction diagram make parallel lines, the transaction is complementary and can go on indefinitely.* It does not matter which way the vectors go (Parent-Parent, Adult-Adult, Child-Child, Parent-Child, Child-Adult) if they are parallel" (Harris, 1969, p. 70). Examples of these transactions are shown in Figure 5.2.

(b) *Uncomplementary, or crossed, transaction* occurs when a message from one ego state (e.g., Parent) receives a response from a different ego

(a) **Parent-Parent**

    S: College students nowadays do not want to work hard for their grades.

    R: Where will it all end?

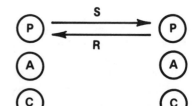

Fig. 5-2a. Parent-parent transaction

(b) **Adult-Adult**

    S: Congratulations on your passing the CPA exam?

    R: Thank you.

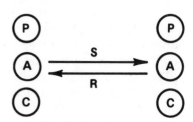

Fig. 5-2b. Adult-adult transaction

(c) **Child-Child**

    S: I don't know how to complete this project.

    R: I always have to be your helper.

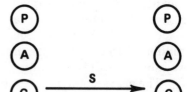

Fig. 5-2c. Child-child transaction

(d) **Parent-Child**

    S: Let me help you with your project.

    R: Gee, I'd like that.

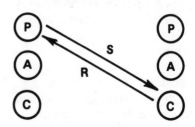

Fig. 5-2d. Parent-child transaction

FIGURE 5.2. Complementary Transactions

(a) **S:** Why are you late today, John?

    R: Don't be so critical.

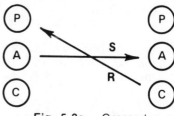

Fig. 5-3a. Crossed transaction

(b) **S:** You stayed away from the meeting again.

    R: If you take care of your problems, you wouldn't notice.

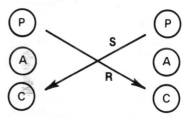

Fig. 5-3b. Crossed transaction

(c) **S:** I have to complete a schedule tonight which is due tomorrow morning.

    R: You will never learn to do things ahead of time.

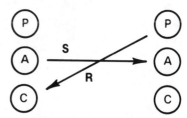

Fig. 5-3c. Crossed transaction

FIGURE 5.3. Uncomplementary Transactions

state (e.g., Adult) than intended. This happens when stimulus and response cross on the P-A-C transaction diagram. As a result, there may be a communication breakdown or conflict. Examples of these transactions are shown in Figure 5.3.

(c) *Ulterior transaction* occurs when the overt stimulus indicates a transaction at one level (Adult-Adult), but the underlying intent of it may place the transaction at another level (Parent-Child). An example of this transaction is given in Figure 5.4.

Although Adult-Adult transaction is the most desirable one, other complementary transactions can operate with some success. For example, if the boss desires to play the role of parent and the subordinate

S: (Subordinate) There may be another way of solving the problem.

R: (Superior) You should try the present method, which worked before, to solve the problem.

Ulterior (U): I don't like your challenging my authority. You must do things exactly in the way I told you to do them.

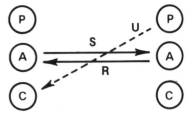

FIGURE 5.4. Ulterior Transaction

desires the role of child, they may develop a relationship that is reasonably effective. But the problem is that the employee fails to grow and mature. Therefore, it has been suggested that Adult-Adult transactions obtain the best results for the individual and the organization.

3. *Life positions.* In a transaction, a person tends to be dominated by one of the four life positions (Harris, 1969). Early in his or her childhood, a person develops a dominant philosophy of relating to others. This tends to remain with the person for a lifetime unless major experiences occur to alter it. These positions can also be used to analyze a series of transactions between two parties. Thus, if an individual is communicating primarily from one ego state, it can correspond to one of these four positions:

| Primarily | | Position |
From	To	Being Assumed
Parent	Child	I'm OK—You're not OK.
Child	Parent	I'm not OK—You're OK.
Adult	Adult	I'm OK—You're OK.
Child	Child	I'm not OK—You're not OK.

In transactional analysis, the emphasis is on authentic communications and relationships. It is expected that as a result of this intervention the organizational members will learn to handle their interpersonal conflict more effectively. It is expected that transactional analysis intervention cannot only affect the way organizational members handle their dyadic conflict but also their intragroup and intergroup conflicts.

A number of companies have used Transactional Analysis. The effectiveness of this technique has yet to be assessed scientifically. Some companies which used this technique reported that it was moderately successful (Rettig & Amano, 1976).

Structural

Several structural interventions are available for the management of interpersonal conflict. Appeal to authority and the use of ombudsmen are two structural arrangements that are presented in this chapter for the management of conflict between two organizational members. These arrangements are necessary to deal with conflicts between two parties when they fail to resolve their disagreements.

Appeal to Authority. Organizations allow members to appeal to a common superior if two or more members, at the same organizational level, fail to resolve their disagreements. The common supervisor can make a decision which will be binding on the two parties involved in conflict and the supervisor has the right to enforce her or his decisions. This system can work effectively if the supervisor is respected by the conflicting individuals, understands the complexity of the problems, and is able to make a good decision. "When the decision-maker cannot understand the issues, or when the conflicting parties do not believe he does or don't respect his authority, his ability to resolve conflict is sharply curtailed. People will not accept the superior's judgement. . . . Of course, hierarchical superiors can resort to their own dominance to force acceptance, but this sharply undermines the efficiency of the system" (Hampton, Summer, & Webber, 1982, p. 642).

Some organizations allow members to appeal to a higher level manager if they feel that the immediate supervisor has not handled a matter fairly. This system may work satisfactorily provided that there are few complaints against the immediate supervisors, the higher level manager devotes adequate time to understand the problem and make a good decision, and the immediate supervisor does not hold a grudge against the complainant. If there are too many complaints against an immediate supervisor, this signals the existence of problems associated with the supervisor. Therefore, the higher level manager should diagnose the problems and take appropriate corrective action. Some organizations allow the lower level members to take their disagreements to grievance committees.

The Ombudsman. This has been an intriguing mechanism for managing conflict in recent years (Silver, 1967). An ombudsman can help the conflicting parties gather more information on the relevant issues so that they can overcome their misunderstanding. He has no authority to make decisions, but he can mediate the disagreements between the two conflicting parties and/or make recommendations.

Some schools are employing ombudsmen to try to resolve teacher-student conflict especially relating to grades, so that formal grievance procedures are not needed. This device may not be useful for resolving major conflicts, but it can be used to deal with routine conflicts that may arise between the superior and a subordinate.

SUMMARY

Interpersonal conflict relates to disagreements, differences, 'or incompatibilities between an individual and his superior(s), subordinates, or peers. There are five styles of handling interpersonal conflict, such as integrating, obliging, dominating, avoiding, and compromising. The model of conflict begins with the antecedent conditions or the sources of conflict and includes behavioral changes, structure formation, decision process, and conflict aftermath.

Although it has been generally accepted that the integrating or problem-solving style is the best for dealing with interpersonal conflict, all the five styles are appropriate depending on situations. For the management of interpersonal conflict, a diagnosis should particularly indicate whether the organizational members are handling their conflict appropriately depending on situations. The factors which affect the styles are personality, bases of power, organizational climate, referent role, and sex. Some of these sources may be altered through appropriate interventions, which in turn will affect the conflict styles of organizational members. The behavioral and structural interventions for the management of interpersonal conflict are transactional analysis, appeal to authority, and ombudsman.

REFERENCES

Aram, J. D., Morgan, C. P., & Esbeck, E. S. (1971). Relation of collaborative interpersonal relationships to individual satisfaction and organizational performance. *Administrative Science Quarterly, 16,* 289–296.

Bell, E. C., & Blakeney, R. N. (1977). Personality correlates of conflict resolution modes. *Human Relations, 30,* 849–857.

Berne, E. (1961). *Transactional analysis in psychotherapy: A systematic individual and social psychiatry.* New York: Grove Press.

Berne, E. (1964). *Games people play: The psychology of human relationships.* New York: Grove Press.

Berne, E. (1972). *What do you say after you say hello? The psychology of human destiny.* New York: Bantam.

Blake, R. R., & Mouton, J. S. (1964). *The managerial grid.* Houston, TX.: Gulf Publishing.

Burke, R. J. (1970). Methods of resolving superior-subordinate conflict: The constructive use of subordinate differences and disagreements. *Organizational Behavior and Human Performance, 5,* 393–411.

Filley, A. C. (1975). *Interpersonal conflict resolution.* Glenview, IL.: Scott, Foresman.

French, J. R. P., Jr., & Raven, B. (1959). The bases of social power. In D. Cartwright (Ed.). *Studies in social power.* Ann Arbor: Institute for Social Research, University of Michigan.

Fry, L. W., Kidron, A. G., Osborn, R. N., & Trafton, R. S. (1980). A constructive replication of the Lawrence and Lorsch conflict resolution methodology. *Journal of Management, 6,* 7–19.

Goldman, R. M. (1966). A theory of conflict processes and organizational offices. *Journal of Conflict Resolution, 10,* 328–343.

Hall, J. (1969). *Conflict management survey: A survey of one's characteristic reaction to and handling conflict between himself and others.* Canoe, TX.: Teleometrics International.

Hampton, D. R., Summer, C. E., & Webber, R. A. (1982). *Organizational behavior and human performance.* Glenview, IL.: Scott, Foresman.

Harris, T. A. (1969). *I'm OK—you're OK: A practical guide to transactional analysis.* New York: Harper.

James, M., & Jongeward, D. (1971). *Born to win: Transactional analysis with gestalt experiments.* Reading, MA.: Addison-Wesley.

Jamieson, D. W., & Thomas, K. W. (1974). Power and conflict in the student-teacher relationship. *Journal of Applied Behavioral Science, 10,* 321–336.

Jones, R. E., & Melcher, B. H. (1982). Personality and the preference for modes of conflict resolution. *Human Relations, 35,* 649–658.

Jung, C. G. (1923). *Psychological types.* London: Routledge and Kegan Paul.

Kahn, R. L., Wolfe, D. M., Quinn, P. R., Snoak, J. D., & Rosenthal, R. A. (1964). *Organizational stress: Studies in role conflict and ambiguity.* New York: Wiley.

Kilmann, R. H., & Thomas, K. W. (1975). Interpersonal conflict-handling behavior as reflections of Jungian personality dimensions. *Psychological Reports, 37,* 971–80.

Kilmann, R. H., & Thomas, K. W. (1977). Developing a forced-choice measure of conflict-handling behavior: The "MODE" instrument. *Educational and Psychological Measurement, 37,* 309–325.

Lawrence, P. R., & Lorsch, J. W. (1967). *Organization and environment.* Homewood, IL.: Irwin-Dorsey.

Likert, R. (1967). *The human organization: Its management and value.* New York: McGraw-Hill.

Likert, R., & Likert, J. G. (1976). *New ways of managing conflict.* New York: McGraw-Hill.

Lusch, R. F. (1976). Sources of power: Their impact on intrachannel conflict. *Journal of Marketing Research, 13,* 382–390.

Musser, S. J. (1982). A model for predicting the choice of conflict management strategies by subordinates in high-stakes conflicts. *Organizational Behavior and Human Performance, 29,* 257–269.

Myers, I. B. (1962). *Manual: The Myers-Briggs type indicator.* Princeton, N J.: Educational Testing Service.

Phillips, E., & Cheston, R. (1979). Conflict resolution: What works? *California Management Review, 21*(4), 76–83.

Pondy, L. R. (1967). Organizational conflict: Concepts and models. *Administrative Science Quarterly, 12,* 296–320.

Prein, H. C. M. (1976). Stijlen van conflicthantering [Styles of handling conflict]. *Nederlands Tijdschrift voor de Psychologie, 31,* 321–346.

Putnam, L. L., & Wilson, C. E. (1982). Communicative strategies in organizational conflicts: Reliability and validity of a measurement scale. In M. Burgoon & N. E. Doran (Eds.), *Communication yearbook 6* (pp. 629–652). Beverly Hills CA.: Sage Publications.

Rahim, A. (1980). Some contingencies affecting interpersonal conflict in academia: A multivariate study. *Management International Review, 20* (2), 117–121.

Rahim, M. A. (1983). A measure of styles of handling interpersonal conflict. *Academy of Management Journal, 26,* 368–376.

Raven, B. H., & Kruglanski, A. W. (1970). Conflict and power. In P. Swingle (Ed.), *The structure of conflict* (pp. 69–109). New York: Academic Press.

Renwick, P. A. (1975). Perception and management of superior-subordinate conflict. *Organizational Behavior and Human Performance, 13,* 444–456.

Renwick, P. A. (1977). The effects of sex differences on the perception and management of superior-subordinate conflict: An exploratory study. *Organizational Behavior and Human Performance, 19,* 403–415.

Rettig, J. L., & Amano, M. M. (1976). A survey of ASPA experience with management by objectives, sensitivity training and transactional analysis. *Personal Journal, 55,* 26–29.

Silver, I. (1967). The corporate ombudsman. *Harvard Business Review, 45* (3), 77–87.

Stern, L. W., & Gorman, R. H. (1969). Conflict in distribution channels: An exploration. In L. W. Stern (Ed.), *Distribution channels: Behavioral dimensions.* Boston: Houghton Mifflin.

Terhune, K. W. (1970). The effects of personality in cooperation and conflict. In P. Swingle (Ed.), *The structure of conflict.* New York: Academic Press.

Thomas, K. W. (1976). Conflict and conflict management. In M. D. Dunnette (Ed.), *Handbook of industrial and organizational psychology* (pp. 889–935). Chicago: Rand McNally.

Thomas, K. W., & Kilmann, R. H. (1974). *Thomas-Kilmann conflict MODE instrument.* New York: XICOM.

Thomas, K. W., & Kilmann, R. H. (1978). Comparison of four instruments measuring conflict behavior. *Psychological Reports, 42* 1139–1145.

Walton, R. E., & Dutton, J. M. (1969). The management of interdepartmental conflict: A model and review. *Administrative Science Quarterly, 14,* 73–84.

Walton, R. E., & McKersie, R. B. (1965). *A behavioral theory of labor negotiations: An analysis of a social interaction system.* New York: McGraw-Hill.

6

Intragroup Conflict

Behavioral scientists make extensive use of small groups in the study of organizational behavior and management. There are several reasons for which the study of groups in organizations has received significant attention. First, groups are the building blocks of an organization. Second, groups provide the primary mechanism for the attainment of organizational goals. Third, groups provide psychological and other supports to the individual members.

There are numerous definitions of groups (Shaw, 1971). These definitions have mainly focused on the following criteria: objectives, interaction, and interdependence. In order to make the discussion of conflict within a group meaningful, the definition of a group should include the following:

1. A group must consist of two or more members.
2. The members should be interdependent and interact with each other.
3. The members should work toward the attainment of a common goal(s).

TYPES OF GROUPS

Groups can be classified in several ways. They may be classified as formal and informal. The formal groups are the task or project groups which are formed by the organization. The members of such a group interact to attain their group goals defined by the organization. The informal groups are the friendship groups which are formed primarily to satisfy the social needs of the members.

Fiedler (1967) further classified task groups into three types according to the nature of task interdependencies between group members in attaining their group objectives. The three types of task groups are interacting, coaching, and counteracting.

In an *interacting group*, the performance of a task by a member depends on the completion of the task assigned to another member. A production team on the assembly line, where the output of one worker becomes the input of another worker, is an example of an interacting group.

A *coaching group* is one in which the members perform their functions relatively independently of each other. Examples of this type of group are faculty groups whose members perform their teaching and research functions relatively independent of each other.

A *counteracting group* is composed of persons who work together for the purpose of negotiating and reconciling conflicting opinions and purposes. This type of group is exemplified by a labor-management negotiating team.

The discussion in this chapter mainly relates to interacting and coaching groups. A counteracting group contains two distinct parties, e.g., labor and management or line and staff; therefore, it has been discussed in the next chapter.

Intragroup conflict refers to the disagreement, differences, or incongruencies among the members of a group or its subgroups regarding goals, functions, or activities of the group. Numerous studies on group dynamics were conducted since the completion of the Hawthorne studies, but there was relatively little systematic study on intragroup conflict.

EFFECTS OF INTRAGROUP CONFLICT

Several studies have reported the relationship between intragroup conflict and individual and organizational outcomes. Julian and Perry (1967) in their experimental study found that both quality and quantity of team performance were considerably higher in competitive than cooperative conditions. Hoffman and Maier (1961) found that experimental groups with heterogeneous members and consequent conflicts of interest and opinion produced better solutions to standardized sets of solutions. Pelz and Andrews (1976) found that scientists who were exposed to discussion with differently oriented colleagues tended to be more productive. Blau's (1963) study of two government agencies suggested a negative relationship between competitive behavior and performance in situations of cooperative group norms.

It is generally agreed by the organization theorists that cooperation or lack of conflict generally induces positive relations among group members, but groups may not be able to attain a higher level of performance. Some of these problems have been discussed under "cohesiveness and groupthink," elsewhere in this chapter.

Rahim's (1983) study with a collegiate sample indicated that there was a low to moderate degree of inverse relationship between intragroup conflict and perceptual measures of three dimensions of organizational effectiveness, such as productivity, adaptability, and flexibility. The correlation between intragroup conflict and organizational climate, as measured by Likert's (1967) Profile of Organizational Characteristics, was negative. This possibly indicates that a higher system of management deals with conflict more constructively than a lower system. The study also indicated a moderate negative correlation between intragroup conflict and job satisfaction. Dewar and Werbel (1979) found a weak negative correlation between overall conflict and job satisfaction.

It is quite possible that other individual outcomes are also associated with intragroup conflict. Future studies need to indicate how different types of intragroup conflict (e.g., substantive conflict and affective conflict) affect individual and group outcomes.

MANAGING INTRAGROUP CONFLICT

The management of intragroup conflict involves effectively channeling the energies, expertise, and resources of the group toward the formulation and/or attainment of group goals. Specifically, this involves altering the sources of conflict among the members of a group so that a moderate amount of conflict is attained and maintained and enabling the group members to learn the styles of handling intragroup conflict to deal with various situations. Since the styles of handling conflict were discussed in detail in the previous chapter, this chapter mainly deals with the amount of intragroup conflict. The diagnosis of and intervention in intragroup conflict are discussed as follows.

Diagnosis

The diagnosis of intragroup conflict and the styles of handling such conflict can be performed by such methods as self-report, observation, interviews, and company records. The ROCI-I can be used to measure the amount of conflict in each group. The items of ROCI-II, Form C, can be slightly altered to measure the styles of handling conflict of the group members. A comprehensive diagnosis of intragroup conflict should involve the following *measurements*:

1. The amount of intragroup conflict and the styles of handling such conflict.
2. Factors which affect intragroup conflict and the styles of handling such conflict.
3. The effectiveness of group(s).

The *analysis* of the above diagnostic data should indicate:

1. The amount of intragroup conflict and the styles of handling such conflict in different groups, departments, units, etc. and whether the amount of conflict deviated from the national norms.
2. Relationship between intragroup conflict, the styles of handling such conflict, and their sources.
3. The relationship between the amount of intragroup conflict, the styes of handling such conflict, and group effectiveness.

National Norms

Data for the national norms were collected on the ROCI-I from 1,188 executives, as described before in Chapter 4. Tables 6.1 and 6.2 are prepared on the basis of this sample.

Table 6.1 shows the national percentile norms of these managers. The percentile score of a manager shows his or her relative position on the intragroup conflict scale. For example, a manager scoring at the 60th percentile on this scale is as high or higher than 60 percent of his normative group who responded to the ROCI-I. His or her score is exceeded by only 40 percent on this group.

Table 6.2 shows the sample size *(N)*, means *(M)* (reference group norms), and standard deviations *(SD)* of the intragroup conflict as reported by 1,188 executives, classified by organizational level, functional area, and education, and the results of one-way analyses of variance *(F)*.

The results of one-way analyses of variance show that there were significant differences in the perception of intragroup conflict among the executives of three organizational levels. The lower executives reported more intragroup conflict than top executives, and the top executives reported more than the middle executives. There were no differences in

TABLE 6.1 Managerial Percentile Norms of Intragroup Conflict ($N = 1,188$)

Mean Scores	Percentiles	Mean Scores
5.00		5.00
4.85		4.85
4.70		4.70
4.55		4.55
4.40		4.40
4.25		4.25
4.10		4.10
3.95	99	3.95
3.80	98	3.80
3.65	97	3.65
3.50	96	3.50
3.35	94	3.35
3.20	93	3.20
3.05	90	3.05
2.90	86	2.90
2.75	82	2.75
2.60	74	2.60
2.45	67	2.45
2.30	56	2.30
2.15	41	2.15
2.00	30	2.00
1.85	16	1.85
1.70	9	1.70
1.55	7	1.55
1.40	4	1.40
1.25	2	1.25
1.10	1	1.10
1.00		1.00

the perception of intragroup conflict among these executives classified by functional area and educational categories.

Sources

Groups are affected by a multitude of factors. The diagnosis of intragroup conflict should indicate the factors which are significantly related to intragroup conflict.

Leadership Style. A leader can virtually influence all other variables affecting conflict within a group. Three examples of group conflict and

TABLE 6.2. Managerial Reference Group Norms of Intragroup Conflict (N = 1,188)

Variables	N	M	SD	F
Organizational Level				6.23*
Top	196	2.33	.5229	
Middle	407	2.28	.5002	
Lower	547	2.41	.6300	
Functional Area				0.94
Production	216	2.38	.5797	
Marketing	27	2.34	.5656	
Finance & Accounting	36	2.24	.6202	
Personnel	24	2.18	.5391	
General Management	252	2.36	.5522	
R&D	198	2.40	.5875	
Engineering	196	2.39	.5784	
Other	214	2.32	.5864	
Education				1.39
High school	136	2.41	.6257	
2-year college	231	2.39	.6095	
Bachelor's degree	529	2.35	.5611	
Master's degree	208	2.31	.5319	
Other	57	2.45	.6091	
Total Sample	1,163	2.36	.5763	

*$p < .05$

their relationship to the leader called situations A, B, and C, were provided by Maier and Verser (1982, p. 153; see Fig. 6.1).

Situation A. This occurs when the leader treats group members differently. Group members may be in conflict with one another if the leader provides favor to one or two members.

Situation B. Intragroup conflict will increase if the group members unite against the leader. This may happen if the leader changes the task structure, schedules, procedures, or removes some privileges, which are perceived by the members as unfair and/or unfavorable.

Situation C. This represents a split in the group. Differences in status, work interest, office space, etc. can encourage the formation of subgroups and conflict among them and the leader.

It should be emphasized that leadership style as a source of intragroup conflict has not been exclusively established through empirical studies. However, it can be hypothesized that a more directive style of leadership generates conflict, while a relations-oriented style provides for its reduction. Likert and Likert (1976) persuasively argue and

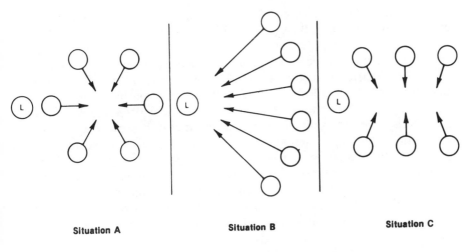

Situation A   Situation B   Situation C

FIGURE 6.1 Three Sources of Intragroup Conflict

provide some evidence that a leadership style based upon System IV can provide for a more functional management of conflict than Systems I, II, or III. Likert (1967) classified his systems I, II, III, and IV as exploitive-authoritative, benevolent-authoritative, consultative, and participative organizations, respectively.

Leadership can influence other variables, such as task structure, group composition, size, etc., which affect the amount of intragroup conflict and the styles of handling conflict by the group members. These variables are discussed as follows.

Task Structure. This represents the extent to which the task is simple (routine) or complex (nonroutine). If a task is routine, it is likely to have clearly defined goals, methods or procedures for doing the task, and have a verifiable correct solution(s). Nonroutine tasks are not well-defined and do not have verifiable correct solutions.

As discussed by House (1971), in simple, routine, and structured tasks, a considerate or supportive leadership style may be more closely related to high job satisfaction and performance than a more directive leadership style. In this situation, there is a lower possibility of conflict between the boss and subordinates. On the other hand, in less structured tasks, subordinates appreciate more direction by their immediate supervisor. In general there is a greater possibility of interpersonal conflict between the superior and subordinates when the task is complex or nonroutine than when the task is simple or routine.

Several studies reported the leadership-task-conflict interaction effects on performance. Bass (1960), Fiedler (1967), and Torrance (1954) asserted that groups under tension and stress perform better under task-oriented leaders. A review of several studies (e.g., Oaklander & Fleishman, 1964; Schriesheim & Murphy, 1976) by Katz (1977, p. 269) showed that, while structuring leadership tends to be more positively related to performance under conditions of high stress, the consideration leadership tends to be positively related to performance under low stress. Katz's (1977) field and experimental studies showed "that initiating-structure was directly related to performance more significantly when high affective conflict was present. Thus, the moderating influence of affective conflict on the effectiveness of structuring leadership was upheld for individuals performing a routine task in laboratory experiment as well as for the more complex and somewhat autonomous tasks performed by the individuals in the field setting" (p. 281).

Group Composition. If a group is composed of individuals with too diverse interpersonal styles, attitudes, values, and interests, the members will have divergent perspectives toward group and organizational goals. In this situation, the members will experience undesirable interpersonal conflict and will have a difficult time in attaining synergistic solutions to the group problems. Rahim's (1979) experimental study found intragroup conflict to be significantly less in homogeneous than heterogeneous groups. However, in organizations where roles are more standardized, the association between conflict and heterogeneity may not be significant (Becker & Geer, 1960). Hall and Williams (1966) found that whereas established groups responded to conflict creatively, the ad hoc groups resolved conflict throught compromise procedures.

A change in group membership can intensify conflict (Kelly, 1974, p. 565). When a new member joins the group, group stability may be disrupted. The manager of a group can affect group composition and conflict by selecting a newcomer for differing attitudes, backgrounds, and experiences.

Size. The size of a group can affect group processes and conflict. As a group grows, potential for conflict increases. Several studies found a positive relationship between group size and dissatisfaction and tension (Corwin, 1969; Hackman & Vidmar, 1970). A large group generally encourages the formation of subgroups each with its informal leader. Some of these subgroups may engage in conflict unless the formal leader follows a more directive and structured approach.

Cohesiveness and Groupthink. One of the major liabilities of a group is that one or more individuals may be forced to conform to the mode of thinking of their majority group members. Asch's (1951) study found that individuals under group pressure will change their opinions about highly objective matters. In a cohesive group, there is a greater possibility that individual members will unwillingly censor their opinions in order to avoid conflict and stay together on all important issues. Janis (1971) used the term "groupthink" as a convenient "way to refer to the mode of thinking that persons engage in when *concurrence-seeking* becomes so dominant in a cohesive ingroup that it tends to override realistic appraisal of alternative course of action" (p. 43).

The victims of groupthink attempt to avoid being too critical of the ideas of their superiors, peers, or subordinates. The group members "adopt a soft line of criticism, even in their own thinking. At their meetings, all the members are amiable and seek complete concurrence on every important issue, with no bickering or conflict to spoil the cozy, 'we-feeling' atmosphere" (Janis, 1971, p. 43). Janis (1971) identified the following eight main symptoms of groupthink which reduce intragroup conflict:

1. *Invulnerability.* Most or all the members of the ingroup share an *illusion* of invulnerability that provides for them some degree of reassurance about obvious dangers and leads them to become overoptimistic and willing to take extraordinary risks.
2. *Rationale.* Victims of groupthink ignore warnings; they also collectively construct rationalizations in order to discount warnings and other forms of negative feedback that, taken seriously, might lead the group members to reconsider their assumptions each time they recommit themselves to past decisions.
3. *Morality.* Victims of groupthink believe unquestionably in the inherent morality of their ingroup; this belief inclines the members to ignore the ethical or moral consequences of their decisions.
4. *Stereotypes.* Victims of groupthink hold stereotyped views of the leaders of enemy groups: they are so evil that genuine attempts at negotiating differences with them are unwarranted, or they are too weak or too stupid to deal effectively with whatever attempts the ingroup makes to defeat their purposes, no matter how risky the attempts are.
5. *Pressure.* Victims of groupthink apply direct pressure to any individual who momentarily expresses doubts about any of the group's shared illusions or who questions the validity of the arguments supporting a policy alternative favored by the majority.
6. *Self-Censorship.* Victims of groupthink avoid deviating from what

appears to be group consensus; they keep silent about their misgivings and even minimize to themselves the importance of their doubts.

7. *Unanimity*. Victims of groupthink share an *illusion* of unanimity within the group concerning almost all judgements expressed by members who speak in favor of the majority view.

8. *Mindguards*. Victims of groupthink sometimes appoint themselves as mindguards to protect the leader and fellow members from adverse information that might break the complacency they shared about the effectiveness and morality of past decisions (pp. 44, 46, 74).

External Threats. The proposition that external conflict increases internal cohesion is an old one. Coser (1956, p. 87), in his Proposition No. 9, suggested that conflict with outgroups increases ingroup cohesion. After an exhaustive review of the theoretical formulations and empirical tests of this proposition, Stein (1976) concluded the following:

> ... there is a clear convergence in the literature in both the specific studies and in the various disciplines, that suggests that external conflict does increase internal cohesion under certain conditions. (p. 165)

Under external threats, group members temporarily put aside their differences and unite against the common enemy. The ingroup often develops stereotypes against the outgroup to justify the conflict and its causes. Bass (1965, pp. 333–34), Blake and Mouton (1961) and others found in their experiments that all groups (in conflict) rated themselves better than the other groups. As a result, conflicts among the members of a group are reduced significantly when the members perceive their group to be in conflict with another group (Sherif, 1958; Sherif, Harvey, White, Hood, & Sherif, 1961). In order for external conflict to reduce intragroup conflict, the following conditions must be satisfied (Stein, 1976):

1. The external conflict needs to involve some threat.
2. [The external conflict must] affect the entire group and all its members equally and indiscriminately, and involve a solution, (at least there must be a useful purpose in group efforts regarding the threat).
3. The group needs to have been an ongoing one with some pre-existing cohesion or consensus, and to have a leadership that can authoritatively enforce cohesion (especially if all the members of the group do not feel the threat).
4. The group must be able to deal with the external conflict, and to provide emotional comfort and support to its members. (p. 165)

External conflict may not reduce intragroup conflict if the external aggressor can tactfully split a subset of the group from the rest of the group members and create dissension and distrust leading one subgroup to blame others (Kretch, Crutchfield, & Ballachy, 1962, p. 450). In such a situation conflict within a group may be increased rather than reduced. Another factor of equal importance for intragroup conflict is the conflict aftermath, i.e., whether the group wins or losses. The losing group may experience more tension and may reassess its strategies or composition. This may lead to an upset in its internal relationships, e.g., change in leadership and undermining of group cohesiveness. In the winning group the amount of conflict may decrease and the group cohesiveness may increase.

A diagnosis of intragroup conflict should particularly indicate whether there is too little, too much, or a moderate amount of conflict and whether conflict is handled by the group members effectively. A diagnosis should also indicate the functional and/or dysfunctional aspects of intragroup conflict in an organization. Based on this information, an intervention decision can be made.

Intervention

The behavioral and structural interventions recommended for managing intragroup conflict follow.

Behavioral

Two organization development techniques, such as team building and role negotiation, have been presented as behavioral interventions which can be used to manage intragroup conflict.

Team Building. This can be viewed as an extension of organization development intervention, such as sensitivity training or T-group. Team building puts emphasis on group learning rather than individual learning as in the case of T-group. Team building is a planned strategy to bring about changes in the attitudes and behavior of the members of an organizational group (or team), whether permanent or temporary, to improve the group's overall effectiveness. A team building exercise may be designed to enable the members to learn the styles of handling conflict and their appropriate uses. The intervention should also enable the group leader and members to become aware of the symptoms of groupthink and make appropriate changes in the group structure and process to remedy them. A team building discussion should enable the group to attain the following (Beckhard, 1972, p. 24):

1. To formulate new and/or revise the existing goals.
2. To formulate and/or revise and allocate tasks to group members to attain the revised goals.
3. To examine the effectiveness of group processes (such as communication, leadership, motivaton).
4. To examine the interpersonal relationships among group members.

Team building, used inappropriately, may have dysfunctional consequences. For example, "the development of a team that results in high conformity may be more dysfunctional than having the existence of conflict" (Bobbitt, Breinholt, Doktor, & McNaul, 1978, p. 339).

To guard against high cohesiveness and groupthink, which may result from team building intervention, the following steps, adapted from Janis (1971, p. 76), may be useful. (1) The leader may encourage each member to evaluate the group decisions critically. The leader should legitimize this practice by accepting some criticisms of his own behavior. (2) The leader should refrain from stating his or her preference to a problem solution when the problem is being discussed by the members. (3) The group should split into several subgroups to work on the same problem, each under a different leader. The separate solutions prepared by the subgroups should be integrated by the members of the group or the representatives of the subgroups.

A plan for the implementation of the solutions should be prepared and several persons should be assigned the responsibilities for implementation. A tentative date(s) for the evaluation of the implementation should also be decided upon.

Team building is very similar to problem-solving intervention which has been discussed in connection with intervention in intergroup conflict. Team building helps the participants to learn the integrative or collaborative style of behavior in handling disagreements.

Role Negotiation. Another technique that can be effectively used with team building to manage intragroup conflict is Harrison's (1972) role negotiation. This technique is useful when intragroup conflict results form the role ambiguities of the group members. An exercise for role negotiation has been developed by Hall, Bowen, Lewicki, and Hall (1975, pp. 224–25). However, the effects of role negotiation on intragroup conflict and effectiveness have not yet been evaluated.

Structural

Unlike behavioral intervention, such as organization development, systematic structural interventions are not available for the management of intragroup conflict. In the following paragraphs several structural changes, which a manager can make to manage intragroup conflict, are presented.

The reduction of intragroup conflict does not appear to be a problem. Conflict may be reduced by making a group more cohesive and homogeneous through interventions of organizational development. If the manager of a group finds that there is less than adequate amount of conflict within his group, he undertakes the difficult task of increasing conflict through structural changes.

One of the potential stategies available to a manager to generate or intensify conflict is to change group membership. When a new member joins a group, the level of conflict may be significantly affected if the newcomer is specifically selected for her or his differing beliefs, training, and experiences. The manager can reduce conflict by transferring one or more conflicting members to other units. This should not be done unless the styles for handling conflict by the members in question are clearly dysfunctional.

The level of conflict may also be altered by changing the group size. The potential for conflict increases as the size of the group is increased. The administrator of a group can change the level of conflict by altering difficulty and variability of the task. The amount of conflict may be reduced by redefining and restructuring tasks, and reducing the inter-relationships among tasks performed by different members. The group leader can also affect the amount of conflict by altering the reward system. A reward system based on performance can generate productive competition and conflict among group members which can increase group effectiveness. The amount of intragroup conflict can be affected by the group leader by altering the rules and procedures and appeals system.

SUMMARY

A group was defined as consisting of two or more members who are interdependent and interact with each other and work toward the attainment of common goals. Groups can be classified as formal and informal. The formal or task groups have been classified as interacting, coaching, and counteracting groups.

The diagnosis of intragroup conflict involves the measurement of the amount of intragroup conflict, the styles of handling intragroup conflict, sources of conflict, and the effectiveness of the group(s). The analysis of diagnostic data should indicate the amount of intragroup conflict and the styles of handling such conflict in each group, department, unit, etc. and whether conflict deviated from the national norms, relationship between conflict and their sources, and between conflict and group effectiveness. There are various antecedent conditions or sources of intragroup conflict, such as leadership style, task structure, group composition, cohesiveness and groupthink, and external threats. These sources of conflict may be altered to reduce or increase intragroup conflict.

Organization development techniques, such as team building and role negotiation, may be used to manage intragroup conflict effectively. Structural interventions designed to manage intragroup conflict include increasing or reducing the size of the group, transferring or exchanging group members, bringing new membership into the group, redefining and restructuring tasks, and altering the reward system, rules and procedures, and appeals system.

REFERENCES

Asch, S. E. (1951). Effects of group pressure on the modification and distortion on judgements. In H. G. Guetzkow (Ed.), *Groups, leadership and men* (pp. 174–183). Pittsburgh: Carnegie Press.

Bass, B. M. (1960). *Leadership, psychology, and organizational behavior*. New York: Harper.

Bass, B.M. (1965). *Organizational psychology*. Boston: Allyn and Bacon.

Becker, H., & Geer, B. (1960). Latent culture: A note on the theory of latent social roles. *Administrative Science Quarterly, 5*, 304–313.

Beckhard, R. (1972). Optimizing team-building efforts. *Journal of Contemporary Business, 1*(3), 23–32.

Blake, R. R., & Mouton, J. S. (1961). Reactions to intergroup competition under win-lose conditions. *Management Science, 7*, 420–435.

Blau, P. M. (1955). *The dynamics of bureaucracy: A study of interpersonal relations in two government agencies* (Rev. ed.). Chicago: University of Chicago Press.

Bobbit, H. R., Jr., Breinholt, R. H., Doktor, R. H., & McNaul, J. P. (1978). *Organizational behavior: Understanding and prediction* (2nd ed.). Englewood Cliffs, N.J.: Prentice-Hall.

Corwin, R. G. (1969). Patterns of organizational conflict. *Administrative Science Quarterly, 14*, 507–520.

Coser, L. A. (1956). *The functions of social conflict*. Glencoe, IL.: Free Press.

Dewar, R., & Werbel, J. (1979). Universalistic and contingency predictions of employee satisfaction and conflict. *Administrative Science Quarterly, 24*, 426–448.

Fiedler, F. E. (1967). *A theory of leadership effectiveness*. New York: McGraw-Hill.

Hackman, J. R., & Vidmar, N. (1970). Effects of size and task type in group performance and member reactions. *Sociometry, 33*, 37–54.

Hall, J., & Williams, M. S. (1966). A comparison of decision-making performances in established and ad-hoc groups. *Journal of Personality and Social Psychology, 3*, 214–222.

Hall, D. T., Bowen, D. D., Lewicki, R. J., & Hall, F. S. (1975). *Experiences in management and organizational behavior.* Chicago: St. Clair Press.

Harrison, R. (1972). Role negotiation: A toughminded approach to team development. In W. W. Burke & H. A. Hornstein (Eds.), *The social technology of organization development.* La Jolla, CA.: University Associates.

Hoffman, L. R., & Maier, N. R. F. (1961). Quality and acceptance of problem solution by members of homogeneous and heterogeneous groups. *Journal of Abnormal and Social Psychology, 62*, 401–407.

House, R. (1971). A path-goal theory of leadership effectiveness. *Administrative Science Quarterly, 16*, 321–338.

Janis, I. L. (1971). Groupthink. *Psychology Today,* November, pp. 43–44; 46; 74–76.

Julian, J. W., & Perry, F. A. (1967). Cooperation contrasted with intra-group and inter-group competition. *Sociometry, 30*, 79–90.

Katz, R. (1977). The influence of group conflict on leadership effectiveness. *Organizational Behavior and Human Performance, 20*, 265–286.

Kelly, J. (1974). *Organizational behavior* (Rev. ed.). Homewood, IL.: Irwin.

Kretch, D., Crutchfield, R. S., & Ballachey, E. L. (1962). *Individual in society: A textbook of social psychology.* New York: McGraw-Hill.

Likert, R. (1967). *The human organization: Its management and value.* New York: McGraw-Hill.

Likert, R., & Likert, J. G. (1976). *New ways of managing conflict.* New York: McGraw-Hill.

Maier, N. R. F., & Verser, G. C. (1982). *Psychology in industrial organizations* (4th ed.). Boston: Houghton Mifflin.

Oaklander, H., & Fleishman, E. A. (1964). Patterns of leadership related to organizational stress in hospital settings. *Administrative Science Quarterly, 8*, 520–532.

Pelz, D. C., & Andrews, F. M. (1976). *Scientists in organizations: Productive climates for research and development.* New York: Wiley.

Rahim, A. (1979). The management of intraorganizational conflicts: A laboratory study with organization design. *Management International Review, 19* (1), 97–106.

Rahim, M. A. (1983). *Rahim organizational conflict inventories: Professional manual.* Palo Alto, CA.: Consulting Psychologists Press.

Schriesheim, C., & Murphy, C. (1976). Relationships between leader behavior and subordinate performance: A test of some situational moderators. *Journal of Applied Psychology, 61*, 634–641.

Shaw, M. E. (1971). *Group dynamics: The psychology of small group behavior.* New York: McGraw-Hill.

Sherif, M. (1958). Superordinate goals in the reduction of intergroup conflict. *American Journal of Sociology, 63*, 349–356.

Sherif, M., Harvey, O. J., White, B. J., Hood, W. R., & Sherif, C. W. (1961). *Intergroup conflict and cooperation: The robbers cave experiment.* Norman: Institute of Group Relations, University of Oklahoma.

Stein, A. A. (1976). Conflict and cohesion: A review of the literature. *Journal of Conflict Resolution, 20,* 143–172.

Torrance, E. P. (1954). The behavior of small groups under the stress of conditions of survival. *American Sociological Review, 19,* 751–755.

7

Intergroup Conflict

It was suggested by some researchers that intergroup conflict is inevitable in complex organizations (Lawrence & Lorsch, 1967; Walton & Dutton, 1969). Complex organizations create different subsystems with homogeneous tasks and distinct goals in order to increase overall organizational effectiveness. Although these subsystems develop distinct norms, orientations, and attitudes, they are required to work with each other for the attainment of organizational goals. This interdependence of the subsystems on tasks, resources, and information, and the heterogeneity among them often are the major generators of conflict between two or more subsystems. "In complex organizations having differentiated subsystems with different goals, norms, and orientations, it appeared that intergroup conflict would be an inevitable part of organizational life" (Lawrence & Lorsch, 1967, p. 42).

Some of the classic examples of organizational intergroup conflict are between line and staff manufacturing and sales production and maintenance, and headquarters and field staffs.

DYNAMICS OF INTERGROUP CONFLICT

Chapter 5 presented a model of organizational conflict. This model requires further analysis for intergroup conflict since this type of conflict displays certain unique patterns.

Studies by Bass (1965), Blake and Mouton (1961), Campbell (1967), Sherif (1958) and others present a highly consistent pattern of what happens when two groups engage in conflict. The following process takes place within and between the conflicting groups.

Behavioral Changes

When intergroup conflict of win-lose orientation occurs, competition between members within each group is reduced. The group members tend to conform to the group norm more and become loyal to the group. Under external threats, the members of the ingroup will play down their disagreements and unite against the outgroup. In other words, an increase in the intergroup conflict may reduce intragroup conflict (see Chapter 6).

One of the possible consequences of win-lose intergroup conflict is that it creates significant distortions in the judgment and perceptual processes of the conflicting groups. The judgmental and perceptual distortions become progressively greater. The work of one's group is seen as superior to that of the opposing group. The members of the ingroup perceive the members of the other group as enemies, and they describe each other in terms of negative stereotypes.

Intergroup conflict may result in the emergence of autocratic leaders. "All too often it is the aggressive person or the ones who express themselves clearly and well who take over. Sometimes those who like fights emerge in leadership positions. Those members who can provide the best leadership and the most skillful leadership processes often are submerged along with the questioning and sounder thinking which they would foster" (Likert & Likert, 1976, p. 61). The new leader(s) is well accepted by the group and is perceived as friendly and perceptive in the analysis of the other group's information.

Structure Formation

The new leader may establish a power structure quickly. Emphasis on task attainment is increased together with the emergence of a greater degree of formality and structure.

A structure of interaction is formulated which discourages free exchange of information. Rules and regulations are established prohibiting intergroup communication. All information is screened by group leadership before dissemination.

Decision Process

The groups establish the medium of negotiation which are usually bargaining, ultimatums, and negotiable demands. These result in further rationing of information, or deliberate distortion of facts. Contacts with other groups become formal, rigid, and carefully defined.

Conflict Aftermath

If bargaining is exclusively utilized as a method of conflict resolution, there is a possibility that both groups will perceive themselves as
partly losers after the cessation of conflict. Such a situation often occurs
after a labor-management conflict is resolved.

If a third party imposes a solution on the conflicting groups, there is
a possibility that a victor and a vanquished will be created. The losing
group may reassess and change its strategies and structure to deal with
the other group.

The model discussed above indicates that the outcomes of win-lose
type of intergroup conflict will probably be dysfunctional for the
organization. The following section discusses the effects of intergroup
conflict on individual and organizational outcomes.

EFFECTS OF INTERGROUP CONFLICT

Some of the effects of intergroup conflict were discussed in the
dynamics of intergroup conflict. Walton and Dutton's (1969) literature
review suggested that the consequences of intergroup conflict can be both

TABLE 7.1. Consequences of Interunit Conflict

Attributes of conflictful lateral relationships	Illustrative consequences
Competition in general	Motivates or debilitates
	Provides checks and balances
Concealment and distortion	Lowers quality of decisions
Channeled interunit contacts	Enhances stability in the system
Rigidity, formality in decision procedures	Enhances stability in the system
	Lowers adaptability to change
Appeals to superiors for decisions	Provides more contact for superiors
	May increase or decrease quality of decisions
Decreased rate of interunit interaction	Hinders coordination and implementation of tasks
Low trust, suspicion, hostility	Psychological strain and turnover of personnel or decrease in individual performance.

functional and dysfunctional, depending on the attributes of conflictful lateral relationships. Some of these relations are shown in Table 7.1.

Table 7.1 shows that whether conflict will be harmful or helpful depends on the nature of specific conflict relationships and the tasks involved. Several earlier studies provided some support to the consequences of interunit conflict presented by Walton and Dutton (e.g., Seiler, 1963; Dalton, 1959). However, further comparative studies are needed to check the validity of these consequences.

Julian and Perry's (1967) experimental study found that groups in competitive condition increased quality and quantity of their output more than the groups under cooperative conditions.

It may be assumed from the above discussion that intergroup conflict may be associated with job dissatisfaction and tension and anxiety on the part of the organizational members. The effects of intergroup conflict on effectiveness have not been properly investigated. Many of the assertions made by researchers are just judgmental. The following section discusses how intergroup confict can be managed effectively.

MANAGING INTERGROUP CONFLICT

The management of intergroup conflict involves channeling the energies, expertise, and resources of the members of conflicting groups for synergistic solutions to their common problems or attainment of overall organizational goals. The diagnosis and intervention for managing intergroup conflict are as follows.

Diagnosis

The diagnosis of intergroup conflict can be performed by means of interviews, observation, company records, and the perceptions of the organizational members. The ROCI-I may be used to measure the amount of intergroup conflict in an organization. If it is needed to measure the amount of conflict between two specific departments, such as production and marketing, the members of production may be asked to respond to the intergroup conflict items to indicate how much conflict they think exists between their department and the marketing department. The members of the marketing department may be asked to indicate how much conflict they think exists between their department and the production department. The items of the ROCI-II, Form C, may be appropriately altered to measure the styles used by the members in handling their intergroup conflict. For example, the item, "I try to investigate an issue with my peers to find a solution acceptable to our department," may be altered to, "I try to investigate an issue with the members of the marketing department to find a solution acceptable to us," to measure how integrating the members of the production department are in handling their conflict with the marketing department.

DuBrin (1972, pp. 213-14) has suggested a way of utilizing the judgments of the administrators to prepare a matrix to understand the location of intergroup conflict. Preparation of this matrix requires the judgment of the chief executive officer (CEO) of an organization about the conflict that exists between the head of each unit and the head of every other unit. The CEO should make proper judgments about interdepartmental conflict after discussing the problem with staff experts in small groups. In Table 7.2 conflict between each department and every other department has been rated. The head of the production department, in this case, is perceived by top management as being in frequent conflict with four department heads. The preparation of the matrix is an exercise by which the top management becomes more conscious about intergroup conflict.

A comprehensive diagnosis of intergroup conflict should include the *measurement* of the following:

1. The amount of conflict that exists between two specific groups.
2. The styles of handling conflict of the ingroup members with the outgroup members.
3. The sources of intergroup conflict.
4. The effectiveness of intergroup relations.

TABLE 7.2. The Conflict Matrix

	Mkt	Prd	QC	Eng	Fnc	Sys	Psn
1. Marketing		−	0	−	−	−	−
2. Production	−		+	+	+	−	+
3. Quality Control	0	+		0	+	+	+
4. Engineering	−	+	+		−	0	+
5. Finance	−	+	+	−		+	+
6. Systems	−	−	−	0	+		+
7. Personnel	−	+	+	+	+	+	
Conflict Index	5	2	1	2	2	2	1

Code: + means better than average cooperation
  0 means normal, average, typical cooperation
  − means lack of cooperation, frequent conflict
  Conflict Index: number of other departments with which that department is in conflict.

The *analysis* of the above diagnostic data should indicate:

1. The amount(s) of intergroup conflict and whether it deviated from the national norm(s) significantly.
2. The relationship between the amount of intergroup conflict, styles of handling such conflict, and the sources of conflict.
3. Relationships between intergroup conflict, the styles of handling such conflict, and the effectiveness of intergroup relations.

National Norms

The data for the preparation of national norms were collected from 1,188 executives, as described in Chapter 3. Table 7.3 shows the national percentile norms of these executives.

Table 7.4 shows the sample size *(N)*, means *(M)* (reference group norms), standard deviations *(SD)* of intergroup conflict classified by organizational levels, functional areas, and educational categories, and the results of one-way analyses of variance *(F)* . The results of one-way analyses of variance show that there were significant differences in the perception of intergroup conflict among the executives of the three organizational levels, functional areas, and educational categories. In particular, the relationship between organizational level and intergroup conflict shows that as the organizational level increases, the perceptions of intergroup conflict reduces.

Sources

The sources of intergroup conflict are mainly structural. The diagnosis of intergroup conflict should identify these sources, which can be altered to attain and maintain a moderate amount of conflict.

System Differentiation. Complex organizations develop differentiated subsystems to attain overall objectives effectively. Differentiated subsystems develop distinct functions, objectives, and norms and compete with each other for resources, power, and status (Seiler, 1963; or Walton & Dutton, 1969). Lawrence and Lorsch (1967) found that subsystems develop different types of internal structures—the formality of structure, time, goal, and interpersonal orientations—to respond to their relevant subenvironments. This heterogeneity in the internal structures of subsystems has important implications regarding the amount of interdepartmental conflict which may arise. Manheim's (1960) experimental study found intergroup hostility "to vary directly with the number of differences between the groups" (p. 426). Smith (1966) found interlevel conflicts to result from difficulties of communication, differences in

TABLE 7.3. Managerial Percentile Norms of Intergroup Conflict ($N = 1,188$)

Mean Scores	Percentiles	Mean Scores
5.00		5.00
4.85		4.85
4.70		4.70
4.55		4.55
4.40		4.40
4.25	99	4.25
4.10	98	4.10
3.95	97	3.95
3.80	95	3.80
3.65	93	3.65
3.50	91	3.50
3.35	87	3.35
3.20	83	3.20
3.05	79	3.05
2.90	74	2.90
2.75	65	2.75
2.60	57	2.60
2.45	53	2.45
2.30	47	2.30
2.15	36	2.15
2.00	28	2.00
1.85	13	1.85
1.70	8	1.70
1.55	4	1.55
1.40	3	1.40
1.25	2	1.25
1.10	1	1.10
1.00		1.00

major interests and goals, and lack of common attitudes and perceptions among members of different levels.

Task Interdependence. Thompson (1967) distinguished among three categories of interdependence: pooled, sequential, and reciprocal. Pooled interdependence refers to a situation where the groups are relatively independent of each other (e.g., the relatively autonomous divisions of a company), but contribute to the attainment of an organization's goals. Sequential interdependence exists where the output of one unit becomes the input of another unit, as in the case of automobile assembly line activities. Under conditions of reciprocal interdependence, the outputs of one group become the input of other groups, in any direction. Sequential

TABLE 7.4. Managerial Reference Group Norms of Intergroup Conflict
($N = 1,188$)

Variables	N	M	SD	F
Organizational Level				25.94*
Top	196	2.30	.6064	
Middle	407	2.54	.6135	
Lower	547	2.69	.7112	
Functional Area				3.99*
Production	216	2.66	.6930	
Marketing	27	2.49	.6594	
Finance & Accounting	36	2.37	.5387	
Personnel	24	2.50	.5773	
General Management	251	2.41	.6535	
R&D	198	2.63	.6845	
Engineering	196	2.66	.6603	
Other	214	2.63	.7036	
Education				2.86*
High school	136	2.59	.7229	
2-year college	231	2.67	.7362	
Bachelor's degree	528	2.55	.6581	
Master's degree	208	2.50	.5821	
Other	57	2.74	.7947	
Total Sample	1,162	2.58	.6786	

*$p < .05$

and reciprocal interdependencies are the major sources of intergroup conflict. White (1961) found that both the drive for departmental autonomy and interdepartmental hostility were the greatest where the interrelationship of tasks was highest. It was suggested that complex interdependencies contribute to a general sense of uncertainty which is a major source of conflict (Crozier, 1964; March & Simon, 1958).

Dependence on Scarce Resources. The subsystems of an organization often must depend on common resources, material and nonmaterial, to attain their respective goals. The greater the perceived dependence on common resources, the greater is the possibility of intergroup conflict (Walton & Dutton, 1969).

Jurisdictional Ambiguity. Jurisdictions over property, authority, and responsibility between two or more subsystems are not always clearly defined. As a result, disputes may arise between purchasing and production or between line and staff to determine the relative contribution to a solution which requires joint effort. Ambiguities often lead to wasteful use of energy and effort between departments over authority, territory, etc. (Seiler, 1963).

Separation of Knowledge from Authority. Some researchers have argued that conflict between line generalists and staff specialists are inherent in the line-staff organization arrangement (Sampson, 1955). Whether this is true or not is uncertain (Belasco & Alutto, 1969); yet there are frequent enough reports about line and staff conflicts to make this a probable causal factor. There are several sources of conflict between line and staff. Staff group members often resent that they are required to understand the line's need, advise them, and justify their own existence (Dalton, 1959). In other words, the success of staff depends on the acceptance of their ideas by line. But the success of line does not necessarily depend on the staff advice, which the line can have when it pleases. This "asymmetrical interdependence" is a major source of conflict.

Sociocultural Differences. Biller and Shanley (1975) suggested that sociocultural differences induce conflict between research and development and other groups. Differences between personality and other behavioral and attitudinal factors and demographics, such as age and sex of the group leaders or representatives may generate intergroup conflict (Walton & McKersie, 1965).

A diagnosis of intergroup conflict should particularly indicate whether there is a moderate amount of this conflict, the functional and dysfunctional aspects of such conflict, and how the ingroup members handle their conflict with outgroup members.

It was emphasized before that a formal diagnosis should precede any intervention strategy designed to manage conflict. But sometimes conflict may become so manifest that a formal diagnosis may not be necessary to understand it. For example, the relationship between two department or division heads may have reached such an impasse that they refuse to communicate with each other except in writing.

Intervention

Several intervention techniques, which can be broadly classified as behavioral and structural, are presented for the management of intergroup conflict. The intervention methods presented here are quite comprehensive and are expected to affect the amount of intergroup conflict and the styles of handling such conflict.

Behavioral

Behavioral interventions, such as organization development, are designed to help the participants to learn mainly collaborative behavior to find the sources of conflict and to arrive at creative solutions. It should be noted that these interventions are useful when the intergroup conflict is strategic rather than frictional or minor. Two intervention strategies, such as problem solving and organizational mirroring, have been presented for managing intergroup conflict. Problem solving is designed to help the members of two groups to learn the integrating style to handle their differences. The organizational mirroring intervention is appropriate when more than two groups are having problems in working together.

Intergroup Problem Solving. Several studies have demonstrated the importance of problem solving in managing intergroup conflict (e.g., Blake, Shepard, & Mouton, 1964; Lawrence & Lorsch, 1967; Likert & Likert, 1976; Schmidt & Tannenbaum, 1960). Problem solving involves four distinct steps.

1. *Problem identification.* The process of problem identification starts with the diagnosis of the nature and sources of intergroup conflict. It includes four parts.
   (a) The representatives or leaders of the two groups and/or the consultant present the diagnostic data to the intergroup members.
   (b) The participants divide into subgroups and meet separately to discuss and identify the intergroup problems which are causing unnecessary conflict.
   (c) The intergroup discusses and integrates the problems identified by the subgroups. It prepares the final list of problems.
   (d) The intergroup ranks the final list of problems.
2. *Problem solution.* This step involves the formulation of alternative solutions to the problems identified above. It involves three sections.
   (a) The intergroup formulates the criteria for solutions.
   (b) The subgroups meet separately and formulate alternative solutions to problems identified in step 1(c) with reference to step 2(a).
   (c) The intergroup discusses and integrates the alternative solutions. It ranks the alternative solutions for each problem.
3. *Implementation plan.* This step in problem solving involves the preparation of a plan for the implementation of the solutions decided above. Five parts are identified.
   (a) The subgroups prepare a plan for implementation (including monitoring of implementation) of the problem solutions.
   (b) The intergroup discusses and analyzes the implementation plans prepared by the subgroups. The intergroup prepares the final plan for implementation (including monitoring of implementation) of the solutions.

(c) The intergroup identifies the problems of implementation. It prepares strategies for overcoming resistance to change.
(d) The intergroup assigns responsibilities for implementations and monitoring implementation to specified individuals.
(e) The intergroup prepares a schedule for follow-up.
4. *Implementation of the plan.* This involves actual implementation of the plan prepared above. It involves the following:
(a) Responsible representatives implement the plan.
(b) Responsible representatives monitor implementation.
5. *Implementation review.* This is the final step in problem solving. The first session is devoted to the attainment of steps 1, 2, and 3. A second session is required to review the results of step 4. In this,
(a) The intergroup meets to evaluate the impact of the plan as specified in step 3(b).
(b) The intergoup may recommend corrective actions if the results of implementation deviate from the standards.
(c) The intergroup decides whether or not to recycle the problem solving process.

It has been observed that the process of problem solving often leads to the emergence of superordinate goals (Blake, Shepard, & Mouton, 1964). The characteristics of superordinate goals are that they are attractive to the members of the conflicting groups, but they cannot be attained by any one group singly. Sherif (1958) has demonstrated that the introduction of a series of superordinate goals is indeed effective in reducing intergroup conflict. Hunger and Stern's (1976) experimental study suggested that "the superordinate goal retards the development of felt conflict even if the frustrating antecedent conditions remain and, although a nonachieved superordinate goal does not reduce or even retard the development of felt conflict, the resultant conflict is no worse than if no superordinate goal had been introduced" (p. 591).

Problem solving can also be used to manage intragroup conflict provided that the group is large where two or more subgroups are engaged in conflict.

Another intervention that has been used to manage intergroup conflict is the confrontation technique. Several variations of confrontation designs have been used in organizations and improved intergroup relations reported (Beckhard, 1967; Blake, Mouton, & Sloma, 1965; Golembiewski & Blumberg, 1968). Confrontation and problem solving use different designs, but they attempt to attain similar objectives—to enable the participants to learn the integrating or collaborating style to deal with intergroup problems synergistically.

Organizational Mirroring. This intervention is designed to improve the relationship among three or more groups (Fordyce & Weil, 1971). Generally the representatives of the work-related groups participate in an intervention exercise to give quick feedback to the host group as to how it is perceived.

The host group which is experiencing conflict with the work-related groups may invite key people from these groups to attend an organizational mirror exercise. The consultant diagnoses the intergroup conflict before the exercise and makes the results ready for presentation. The steps involved in the exercise are eight (Fordyce & Weil, 1971).

1. The manager of the host group explains the objectives of the meeting and the schedule for the exercise.
2. The consultant presents his findings of the conflict diagnosis performed on the participating groups.
3. The members of work-related groups form a"fishbowl" to interpret and discuss the data presented by the consultant. The host group members listen and take notes.
4. The host group members form a "fishbowl" to discuss what they learned from work-related groups. They may ask for clarification from the work-related groups.
5. Subgroups of members of host and work-related groups are formed and asked to identify the significant intergroup problems which must be solved to enhance the host group's effectiveness.
6. The subgroups report the problems identified by them. The participants discuss these problems and prepare a final list for which actions are needed.
7. Action plans and strategies for implementaion are prepared for each problem by subgroups.
8. The intergroup reviews and accepts the action plans and implementation strategies. A tentative date(s) for a follow-up meeting is agreed upon.

This intervention strategy is particularly suitable where the solution of an interface problem requires the collaboration of several work-related groups. The intervention requires careful planning and management for which the service of an efficient consultant is required.

Structural

As discussed before, one of the major sources of intergroup conflict is that there are signficant intedependencies between departments, units or groups. Structural interventions may be made to deal with these interdependencies effectively.

Analysis of Task Interdependence. This intervention involves the analysis of tasks to reduce and/or manage the task interdependencies between two groups effectively. The following steps, appropriately integrated into a problem-solving process, may achieve this objective (Rahim, 1977):

1. The representatives of the conflicting groups engage in identifying and explaining the task items which create interface problems.
2. When the list of interdependent task items is prepared, the participants engage in the process of a qualitative factor analysis of the task items. This will lead to the classification of tasks into several clusters.
3. The task clusters are assigned to the groups on the basis of congruence between the needs of the tasks and the skill, and materials and other resources possessed by the groups necessary to perform these tasks.
4. One or more of the task clusters cannot be assigned to a particular group because no one group has the expertise, resource, or authority to perform the task cluster(s). Integrative teams or committees must be set up consisting of representatives of the conflicting groups to perform these interface tasks. Lawrence and Lorsch (1967) found that in organizations where the departments achieved higher degree of differentiation the use of "integrator" units or individuals facilitated the management of interdepartmental conflict.

Structural changes may also be made by the superior through authoritative command. Intergroup conflict may be increased or reduced by hiring, transferring, or exchanging group members to increase homogeneity/heterogeneity within/between groups. Stern, Sternthal, and Craig (1973) suggested that exchange of members between groups may resolve intergroup conflict by reducing ingroup/outgroup bias. The amount of intergroup conflict may be altered by clarifying and formulating rules and procedures, which affect intergroup relationship; altering the system of communication between groups; developing an appeals system; and providing valid information when the perceptions of the ingroup about the outgroup are distorted.

SUMMARY

Intergroup conflict is inevitable in complex organizations. Some of the classic examples of intergroup conflict in an organizaton are between line and staff, manufacturing and sales, production and maintenance, and headquarters and field staffs. The processes of intergroup conflict follow certain patterns which may not be found in other types of organizational conflict.

The management of intergroup conflict requires the diagnosis of and intervention in conflict. The diagnosis should indicate whether intergroup conflict is at a moderate level, the functional and dysfunctional aspects of such conflict, and the styles of handling conflict of the ingroup with the outgroup members. The sources of intergroup conflict are system differentiation, task interdependency, dependence on scarce resources, jurisdictional ambiguity, separation of knowledge from authority, and sociocultural differences.

Behavioral interventions, such as problem solving, confrontation, and organizational mirroring, have been presented for managing conflict between groups. Structural interventions, such as the analysis of tasks to reduce the task interdependencies, may be used to manage intergroup conflict. Other structural interventions involve hiring, transferring or exchanging group members, clarifying and formulating rules, procedures, developing an appeals system, altering the system of communication, and providing valid information when the perceptions of the ingroup about the outgroup are distorted.

REFERENCES

Bass, B. M. (1965). *Organizational psychology*. Boston: Allyn and Bacon.

Beckhard, R. (1967). The confrontation meeting. *Harvard Business Review, 45*(2), 149–155.

Belasco, J. A., & Alutto, J. A. (1969). Line and staff conflicts: Some empirical insights. *Academy of Management Journal, 12,* 469–477.

Biller, A. D., & Shanley, E. S. (1975). Understanding the conflicts between R&D and other groups. *Research Management, 18(5),* 16–21.

Blake, R. R., & Mouton, J. S. (1961). Reactions to intergroup competition under win-lose conditions. *Management Science, 7,* 420–435.

Blake, R. R., Mouton, J. S., & Sloma, R. L. (1965). The union-management intergroup laboratory: Strategy for resolving intergroup conflict. *Journal of Applied Behavioral Science, 1,* 25–57.

Blake, R. R., Shepard, H. A., & Mouton, J. S. (1964). *Managing intergroup conflict in industry*. Houston, TX.: Gulf Publishing.

Campbell, D. R. (1967). Stereotypes and the perception of group differences. *American Psychologist, 22,* 817–829.

Crozier, M. (1964). *The bureaucratic phenomenon*. Chicago: University of Chicago Press. (Auth. Trans. from French.)

Dalton, M. (1950). Conflicts between staff and line managerial officers. *American Sociological Review, 15,* 342–351.

DuBrin, A. J. (1972). *The practice of managerial psychology: Concepts and methods for manager and organization development.* New York: Pergamon Press.

Fordyce, J. K., & Weil, R. (1971). *Managing with people: A manager's handbook of organization development methods.* Reading, MA.: Addison-Wesley.

Golembiewski, R. T., & Blumberg, A. (1968). The laboratory approach to organizaton change: "Confrontation design." *Academy of Management Journal, 11,* 199–210.

Hunger, J. D., & Stern, L. W. (1976). An assessment of the functionality of the superordinate goals in reducing conflict. *Academy of Management Journal, 19,* 591–605.

Julian, J. W., & Perry, F. A. (1967). Cooperation contrasted with intra-group and inter-group competition. *Sociometry, 30,* 79–90.

Lawrence, P. R., & Lorsch, J. W. (1967). Differentiation and integration in complex organizations. *Administrative Science Quarterly, 12,* 1–47.

Likert, R., & Likert, J. G. (1976). *New ways of managing conflict.* New York: McGraw-Hill.

Manheim, H. L. (1960). Intergroup interaction as related to status and leadership differences between groups. *Sociometry, 23,* 415–427.

March, J. G., & Simon, H. A. (1958). *Organizations.* New York: Wiley.

Rahim, M. A. (1977). The management of organizational intergroup conflict: A contingency model. *Proceedings of the 8th Annual Meeting of the Midwest American Institute for Decision Sciences,* Cleveland: 247–249.

Sampson, R. C. (1955). *The staff role and management: Its creative uses.* New York: Harper.

Schmidt, W. H., & Tannenbaum, R. M. (1960). Management of differences. *Harvard Business Review, 38*(06), 107–115.

Seiler, J. A. (1963). Diagnosing interdepartmental conflict. *Harvard Business Review, 41*(5), 121–132.

Sherif, M. (1958). Superordinate goals in the reduction of intergroup conflict. *American Journal of Sociology, 63,* 349–358.

Smith, C. G. (1966). A comparative analysis of some conditions and consequences of interorganizational conflict. *Adminstrative Science Quarterly, 10,* 504–529.

Stern, L. W., Sternthal, B., & Craig, C. S. (1973). Managing conflict in distribution channels: A laboratory study in distribution channels. *Journal of Marketing Research, 10,* 169–179.

Thompson, J. D. (1967). *Organizations in action.* New York: McGraw-Hill.

Walton, R. E., & Dutton, J. M. (1969). The management of interorganizational conflict: A model and review. *Administrative Science Quarterly, 14,* 73–84.

Walton, R. E., & McKersie, R. B. (1965). *A behavioral theory of labor negotiations: An analysis of a social interaction system.* New York: McGraw-Hill.

White, H. (1961). Management conflict and sociometric struture. *American Journal of Sociology, 67,* 185–199.

8

Epilogue

The study of organization theory is not complete without an analysis of conflict and its management. The classical organization theorists did not appreciate the role that conflict can play in an organization. They assumed conflict to be detrimental to an organization. As a result, they attempted to design organizations to minimize conflict. The human relations movement in the 1930s also emphasized the need to enhance harmony and minimize conflict among organizational members. Whereas the classical organization theorists attempted to reduce conflict by altering the technological system of an organization, the human relationists attempted to reduce it by strengthening its social system. This notion of organizational conflict dominated the management thinking during the first half of this century.

In recent years, a somewhat different set of background assumptions about conflict have come to be endorsed. Organizational conflict is now considered as inevitable and even as a positive indicator of effective management of an organization.

Conflict may be both functional and dysfunctional for an organization. It is functional to the extent to which it results in better solutions to problems or effective attainment of individual, subsystem, or organizational objectives which otherwise would not have been possible. In general, either too little or too much conflict may be dysfunctional for an individual, group, or organization. The relationship between conflict and organizational effectiveness approximates an inverted-U function. Whereas too little conflict may lead to stagnation, too much conflict may lead to confusion and organizational disintegration. A moderate amount of conflict, handled properly, is essential for attaining and maintaining an optimum level of individual, group and organizational effectiveness.

There is no generally accepted definition of social or organizational conflict. Organizational conflict can be defined as an "interactive state" manifested in disagreement, difference, incompatibility within or between social entities, i.e., individual, group, and organization. In order for conflict to take place, it has to exceed the threshold level, i.e., the disagreements or incompatibilities must be serious enough before the parties are drawn to conflict. There are differences in the threshold of conflict awareness or tolerance among individuals or groups. Competition can be distinguished from conflict. It was suggested that competition is a subset of conflict.

Organizational conflict may be classified on the basis of its sources or antecedent conditions. Accordingly, it was classified as affective conflict, conflict of interest, conflict of values, cognitive conflict, and substantive conflict. Conflict can also be classified on the basis of the organizational level at which it may originate, such as individual, interpersonal, group, and intergroup. The classification of conflict based on organizational levels suggests that the analysis at a level can be appropriate depending on the nature of the problem(s).

A DESIGN FOR MANAGING CONFLICT

Organizational conflict must not necessarily be reduced, eliminated, or avoided, but managed to reduce its dysfunctional outcomes and enhance its functional outcomes. The management of organizational conflict involves, in general, the maintenance of a moderate amount of conflict at various levels and enabling the organizational members to learn the five styles for handling interpersonal conflict for dealing with different situations effectively. In other words, a moderate amount of conflict, handled in a proper fashion, may be functional for an organization.

The management of organizational conflict involves the diagnosis of and intervention in conflict. A comprehensive diagnosis involves the measurement of the amount of conflict and the styles of handling interpersonal conflict; the sources of conflict; and individual, group, or organizational effectiveness. The data for the diagnosis should be collected through questionnaires, interviews, and observation. The analysis of diagnostic data should indicate whether conflict at various levels and the styles of handling interpersonal conflict deviated from their corresponding national norms significantly; whether the styles of handling interpersonal conflict are used to deal with different situations effectively; and the relationships of the amount of conflict, conflict styles, and their sources and effectiveness.

Intervention is needed when there is too little or too much of conflict at any level and the organizational members have difficulty in selecting and using the five styles of handling interpersonal conflict to deal with different situations effectively. The analysis of diagnostic data should be studied carefully before designing an intervention strategy. In particular, the sources of conflict which correlate significantly with conflict should be selected for alteration to generate or reduce conflict or to change the styles of handling interpersonal conflict. There are two types of intervention: behavioral and structural.

Management scholars and practitioners have particularly neglected the diagnosis of a problem before intervention. The methodology for a comprehensive diagnosis of organizational conflict was presented in Chapters 4 through 7. Every organization, of course, does not need or can afford to conduct the comprehensive diagnosis presented in this book. But some diagnosis is needed to improve the effectiveness of an intervention.

The national norms of the three types of conflict and the five styles of handling interpersonal conflict have been prepared to help the managers or organizational consultants to decide whether an organization has too little, too much, or a moderate amount of conflict and whether the organizational members are making too little, too much, or a moderate use of the styles of handling interpersonal conflict. It should be noted that the norms are the averages based on the responses of managers from different types of firms. Therefore, they provide some crude indicators of what may be an acceptable level of conflict.

The norms of the styles of handling conflict cannot provide any indication as to whether a style has been appropriately used to deal with a particular situation. In-depth interviews with the organizational members are needed to determine whether they are selecting and using the styles to properly deal with different situations.

Table 8.1 shows the taxonomy for the management of organizational conflict at the individual, interpersonal, group, and intergroup levels discussed throughout the book. Following is a discussion of this taxonomy.

Intrapersonal Conflict

Intrapersonal conflict occurs when a person is required to perform a task which does not match his or her expertise, interests, goals, and

TABLE 8.1. A Taxonomy for the Management of Organizational Conflict

Intrapersonal Conflict

Diagnosis

  Measurement
    1. Amount of intrapersonal conflict
    2. Sources of intrapersonal conflict
    3. Effectiveness of the individual members of an organization

  Analysis
    1. Amount of intrapersonal conflict in various organizational levels, units, departments, or divisions and whether they deviated from the national norms significantly
    2. Relationship between intrapersonal conflict and its sources
    3. Relationship between intrapersonal conflict and individual effectiveness

  Intervention
    1. Technique of role analysis
    2. Job design

  Results
    1. Low to moderate amount of conflict
    2. Greater individual effectiveness

Interpersonal Conflict

Diagnosis

  Measurement
    1. Styles of handling interpersonal conflict used by the organizational members to deal with different situations
    2. Factors which affect the styles of handling conflict
    3. Effectiveness of the individual members of an organization

  Analysis
    1. Styles of handling interpersonal conflict used by members of various units, departments, and divisions, and whether they deviated from the national norms significantly
    2. Whether organizational members are using appropriate styles to deal with different situations effectively
    3. Relationship between styles, situations, and individual effectiveness

  Intervention
    1. Transactional Analysis

TABLE 8.1 *(continued)*

2. Provision for appeal to authority
3. Provision for ombudsman

Results
1. Appropriate selection and use of the five styles of handling interpersonal conflict to deal with different situations
2. Improved communication
3. Greater individual effectiveness

Intragroup Conflict

Diagnosis

Measurement
1. Amount of intragroup conflict and the styles of handling such conflict
2. Factors which affect intragroup conflict and the styles of handling such conflict
3. Effectiveness of groups

Analysis

1. Amount of intragroup conflict and the styles of handling such conflict in different groups, departments, units, etc. and whether the amount of conflict deviated from the national norms
2. Relationship between intragroup conflict, the styles of handling such conflict, and their sources
3. Relationship between the amount of intragroup conflict, the styles of handling such conflict, and group effectiveness

Intervention
1. Team building
2. Role negotiation
3. Structural changes

Results
1. Moderate amount of conflict
2. Improved intragroup relationship
3. Greater group effectiveness

Intergroup Conflict

Diagnosis

Measurement
1. Amount of conflict between two specific groups

TABLE 8.1 *(continued)*

   2. Styles of handling conflict of the ingroup with the outgroup members
   3. Sources of intergroup conflict
   4. Effectiveness of intergroup relations

Analysis
   1. Amount of conflict between two specific groups and whether it deviated from the national norm
   2. Styles of handling conflict of the ingroup with outgroup members
   3. Relationship between intergroup conflict, the styles of handling such conflict, and the effectiveness of intergroup relations

Intervention
   1. Intergroup problem solving
   2. Organizational mirroring
   3. Analysis of task interdependence
   4. Structural changes

Results
   1. Moderate amount of conflict
   2. Greater synergy in intergroup decisions
   3. Improved communication between groups
   4. Better relationship between groups

values. Such conflict also occurs when the role a person expects to perform and the role that is demanded of him by the organization are incongruent. Intrapersonal conflict may lead to job dissatisfaction, tension, absenteeism, and organizational withdrawal. Studies on intrapersonal conflict did not indicate any functional outcome of intrapersonal conflict. Therefore, an attempt may be made to maintain a low to moderate amount of intrapersonal conflict.

The management of intrapersonal conflict involves matching the individual goals and role expectations with the needs of the task and role demand so that the organizational and individual goals can be attained.

The diagnosis of this type of conflict involves the measurement of the amount of intrapersonal conflict, the sources of such conflict, and idividual effectiveness. The sources of intrapersonal conflict are misassignment and goal incongruence, inappropriate demand on capacity, organization structure, supervisory style, and position. These sources may be altered to reduce or generate intrapersonal conflict.

The analysis of diagnostic data should indicate the amount of intrapersonal conflict existing at various organizational levels, units, departments, and divisions, and whether they deviated from the national norms significantly; the relationship between conflict and its sources; and the relationship between intrapersonal conflict and individual effectiveness. At the very least, a diagnosis should indicate whether there is a low, moderate, or high amount of intrapersonal conflict in various levels or units of an organization. A diagnosis should indicate whether there is a need for intervention and the type of intervention needed.

The technique of role analysis and job design are two behavioral and structural interventions, respectively, which can be used to manage intrapersonal conflict. Role analysis may be used to analyze and differentiate individual, group, and intergroup roles and to enable the individuals to deal with tasks and role interdependencies more systematically. Job design is a structural intervention for changing several dimensions of a job for increasing motivation and job satisfaction and reducing dysfunctional intrapersonal conflict.

Interpersonal Conflict

Interpersonal conflict refers to disagreements, differences, or incompatibilities between an individual and his or her superior(s), subordinates, and peers. Chapter 5 presented a model of organizational conflict especially interpersonal, intragroup, and intergroup conflicts. The model begins with the sources of conflict, such as behavioral, structural, and demographic factors. These factors affect the amount of conflict and the styles of handling conflict. The model shows how the behavior and attitudes of the parties are affected during conflict and the consequences of such change on the relationship between parties. If the conflict intensifies, it may lead to structure formation, e.g., the parties may decide to communicate only through writing. As a result of the win-lose conflict, the parties may decide to use a new decision process which is bargaining and negotiation rather than problem solving. The aftermath of conflict may be a feeling of victory or defeat which will affect future conflict resolution methods used by the parties. This model should enable an organizational practitioner to understand the dynamics of conflict and to design appropriate intervention methods to deal with conflict effectively.

There are five styles of handling interpersonal conflict, such as integrating, obliging, dominating, avoiding, and compromising. The literature indicated that the use of problem-solving or integrating style increases job satisfaction but not performance. These studies neglected to investigate the appropriateness of the five styles depending on situations.

It has been suggested that each of these styles is appropriate depending on situations. In general, integrating and to some extent compromising styles are appropriate for handling conflicts involving complex problems, and obliging, dominating, avoiding, and compromising styles are appropriate for dealing with day-to-day or minor problems.

The management of intrapersonal conflict involves enabling the organizational participants to learn the five styles of handling conflict to deal with different conflict situations with superiors, subordinates, and peers effectively.

The diagnosis of interpersonal conflict involves the measurement of the styles of handling interpersonal conflict used by the organizational members to deal with different situations, the factors which affect the styles of handling conflict, and the effectiveness of the individual members of an organization. The factors which affect the styles of handling interpersonal conflict are personality, bases of power, organizational climate, referent role, and sex.

The analysis of data should indicate whether the styles of handling conflict used by the members of various units, departments, or divisions deviated from their corresponding national norms significantly, or whether the styles are appropriately used to deal with different situations. The analysis should also indicate which factors affect significantly the styles of handling conflict, and the relationship between the styles and individual effectiveness.

Intervention is particularly needed if the organizational members have difficulty in selecting and using the five styles of handling interpersonal conflict to deal with different situations effectively. Several intervention methods have been presented for the management of interpersonal conflict. Transactional analysis training is an intervention which is designed to improve communication among the members of an organization and to enhance integrating style and to some extent compromising style, and reduce obliging, dominating, and avoiding styles.

Structural intervention techniques, such as provision for appeal to authority and the ombudsman, are designed to help the organizational members to deal with routine interpersonal conflict. Structural interventions are not designed to alter the styles of handling conflict of organizational members but to enable them to resolve certain minor conflicts quickly.

Intragroup Conflict

This refers to disagreements, differences, or incompatibilities among the members of a group or its subgroups. It is generally agreed by organization theorists that lack of conflict or cooperation enhances positive relationships among group members, but the group members may not be able to attain higher level of performance. Several studies indicate that competitive groups perform better than cooperative ones.

The management of intragroup conflict involves effectively channeling the energies, expertise, and resources of a group in conflict toward the formulation and/or attainment of group goals.

A comprehensive diagnosis of intragroup conflict involves the measurement of the amount of intragroup conflict, styles of handling intragroup conflict, the factors which affect intragroup conflict and the styles of handling such conflict, and the effectiveness of groups. The factors which affect intragroup conflict are leadership style, task structure, group composition, size, cohesiveness and groupthink, and external threats.

The analysis of diagnostic data should indicate the amount of intragroup conflict and the styles of handling such conflict in different groups, departments, units, etc., and whether the amount of intragroup conflict deviated from the national norms significantly; the relationships of intragroup conflict, the styles of handling such conflict, the sources of conflict, and the relationships of the amount of intragroup conflict, the styles of handling such conflict, and group effectiveness.

At the minimum, the diagnosis of intragroup conflict should indicate whether there is too little, too much, or a moderate amount of conflict and whether conflict is handled by the group members effectively.

The behavioral interventions available for the management of intragroup conflict are team building and role negotiation. Team building is designed to enable a group to analyze and redefine its goals, tasks, group processes, and interpersonal relationships. A team building intervention can be used to manage intragroup conflict effectively. Role negotiation is appropriate when conflicts result from the role ambiguities of group members.

Several structural interventions are available to deal with intragroup conflict. Conflict may be reduced by making a group more cohesive and homogeneous through interventions of organization development. A manager can intensify intragroup conflict altering the composition of group members. The amount of conflict may also be altered by changing the group size, task structure, reward system, rules and procedures, and appeals system.

Intergroup Conflict

Intergroup conflict refers to disagreements, differences, or incompatibilities between the members or their representatives of two or more groups. The effects of intergroup conflict can be both functional and dysfunctional, depending on the nature of conflict relationships and the tasks involved.

The management of conflict between two or more groups involves channeling the energies, expertise, and resources of the conflicting groups for synergistic solutions to their common problems or attainment of overall organizational goals.

The diagnosis of intergroup conflict requires the measurement of the amount of conflict between two specific groups, the styles of handling conflict of the ingroup members with outgroup members, the sources of intergroup conflict, and the effectiveness of intergroup relations. The sources of intergroup conflict are system differentiation, task interdependence, dependence on scarce resources, jurisdictional ambiguity, separation of knowledge from authority, and sociocultural differences.

The analysis of diagnostic data should indicate whether the amount of intergroup conflict deviated from the national norms significantly, whether the intergroup conflict is handled effectively, the relationship between the amount of intergroup conflict, the styles of handling such conflict and their sources, and the relationship between intergroup conflict, the styles of handling such conflict, and the effectiveness of intergroup relations. A diagnosis, at the minimum, should indicate whether there is a moderate amount of intergroup conflict and whether the ingroup members are handling their conflict with outgroup members effectively.

The behavioral intervention strategies, such as problem solving and organizational mirroring, have been presented for managing intergroup conflict. The problem solving is designed to help the members of two groups to learn the integrating style to deal with their incompatibilities. The organizational mirroring intervention is appropriate when more than two groups are having problems in working together.

Intergroup conflict often results from interdependence between groups. The analysis of task interdependence is a structural intervention designed to reduce and/or manage the interdependent tasks more effectively. Other structural changes to reduce or generate intergroup conflict are hiring, transferring, or exchanging group members, clarifying and formulating rules and procedures, developing an appeals system, and providing valid information when the perceptions of ingroup about outgroup are distorted.

MEASUREMENT OF CONFLICT

Two instruments have been developed to measure organizational conflict. The Rahim Organizational Conflict Inventory-I has been designed to measure the amount of intrapersonal, intragroup, and intergroup conflicts. The Rahim Organizational Conflict Inventory-II has been designed to measure the styles of handling interpersonal conflict with superior(s) (Form A), subordinates (Form B), and peers (Form C). Some of the items and instructions of this inventory may be altered to measure how a person handles his or her intragroup and intergroup conflicts.

The scales of the two inventories were constructed on the basis of several pilot studies and two separate national studies. The results of the data analysis suggested that the scales have adequate reliability and validity.

The national norms of conflict, reported in Chapters 4 through 7, were prepared on the basis of data from the two national samples collected through the two inventories. The two inventories were primarily developed for the diagnosis of the amount of the three types of conflict and the five styles of handling interpersonal conflict with different parties. As it stands now, the inventories can be used for the diagnosis of organizational conflict, basic research, and teaching.

APPENDIX A

Cases

In this section, two cases have been presented. The names of individuals and companies in these cases have been disguised at the request of the company officials.

The cases should be used to enable the participants in a management workshop to learn how to deal with conflict situations in an organization. In particular, the participants should be encouraged to work on the following aspects of a case:

1. Recognition of the major and minor problem of a company or one or more of its subsystems.
2. Detailed analyses of the above problems.
3. Recommendations for alternative courses of action.

The cases should not be used to demonstrate the superiority of one course of action over another. They should be used to enable the participants to develop their problem-solving skills.

CASE: 1 ALLEN MANUFACTURING CORPORATION

Allen Manufacturing was founded in 1966 by Frank Allen, who personally managed the company until his death in 1972. He was succeeded by his sons Steve, who became the president of the corporation, and Walter, who assumed the position of general manager.

The company manufactures exothermic products for use in steel production, such as fiber mold liners, superimposed consumable hot tops, and exothermic side boards. The manufacturing plant consists of mixing operations, where raw materials are blended in electric powered ribbon mixers, and molding operations, where the mixture is placed into dies and formed as per mold design of the customer. Following the molding operation, the product is transported to the curing area by means of a gasoline powered forklift and placed into the furnace for a period of 4 to 6 hours at 400 degrees Fahrenheit. The product is cooled and transported to the packing area to be packed and shipped.

Production Department

The production department is under the supervision of David Blake, production superintendent. He joined the company in 1964 as a laborer and, subsequently, worked his way through the ranks.

David Blake's assistant is John Donovan, who was hired in 1970 as an assistant quality control manager. He was appointed as David's assistant in 1972 because of his abilities in administrative procedures. Currently John handles all the administrative duties, while David supervises production.

The third in command in production is Donald Nelson, who is the general foreman. His job is to schedule production on a day-to-day basis and to follow it through.

Maintenance Department

The maintenance department is headed by James Seibert, maintenance superintendent. James has been with the company since its inception and is a close personal friend of David Blake. It is James' duty to order replacement parts and perform necessary repairs of company equipment.

James' assistant, Joe Kelly, directly assigns and supervises the maintenance duties. The maintenance department usually receives assignments for maintenance by means of work orders written by one of the production foremen and approved by John Donovan.

Incident I

Don Nelson approached Jim Seibert with, "Our furnaces are in desparate need of repair. They are inconsistent. The ware is constantly being overbaked in certain sections and not baked enough in others."

Jim Seibert's reply was, "We are constantly repairing the furnaces, but with the parts and equipment available we are not able to repair them to your satisfaction. I have been told that funds are not available for the purchase of these parts."

Incident 2

Don Nelson again approached Jim Seibert, "How are we expected to meet our orders if we cannot get our ware to the furnace? Two of our forklifts are out-of-order; and the remaining two, which are in use, are unsafe to operate."

Jim Seibert replied, "You can't expect miracles from my men. They are underpaid and overworked as it is. You will have to get by with the two lifts you are now operating until we get the opportunity to repair the ones in the shop."

When Don Nelson passed this information to his supervisor David Blake, he was told, "I feel that under the circumstances maintenance is doing the best they can. Just give them time."

Dissatisfied with David Blake's answer, Don Nelson decided to take the situation into his own hands and to write a memo to Walter Allen.

To: Walter Allen
From: Donald Nelson
Subject: Unsatisfactory condition of equipment

I feel a problem has arisen in the plant that you should be aware of. We are finding great difficulty in meeting our orders. Our furnaces are not working properly and our forklifts are in deplorable condition. Every time I approach Jim Seibert on the subject I get a poor excuse instead of action.

Upon receipt of the memo, Walter Allen called a meeting with David Blake, John Donovan, Jim Seibert, Don Nelson, and Joe Kelly. All participants at the meeting were free to discuss their respective problems. The results of the meeting were as follows:

1. Jim Seibert was given more freedom in purchasing parts and equipment.
2. It was suggested that Don Nelson submit his orders and complaints to maintenance in the form of written work orders, so that his views would not be put off or overlooked.
3. Through the work order process, David Blake and John Donovan would be made aware of the problems Don Nelson was experiencing.

CASE 2: MINNIS SERVICE

Minnis Service is a TV, appliance, and gas engine repair service which is owned and operated by Minnis retail chain. Minnis Service is an autonomous unit whose manager reports directly to a regional office. The organization structure of Minnis Service is shown in Figure A.1.

It is the policy of Minnis Retail Chain to provide emergency service to the customers. When a customer calls for service on a "warm" refrigerator and there is the danger of losing food, the service call is assigned to the closest appliance technician. Since the calls are not anticipated, the technicians often work overtime. If a technician is called from home for emergency service, he is guaranteed four hours of pay.

All associates are asked on their employment application if they will be willing to work outside "normal working hours." Normal working hours are 8:00 A.M to 4:30 P.M. All associates are allowed two 15-minute breaks and a 30-minute lunch per day. They have been instructed to take the mid-morning, mid-afternoon, and lunch breaks by 1:00 P.M. at the latest. Therefore, lunch covers the 30-minute break required by labor laws for workers who work in excess of five hours per day.

Incident I

About three months ago, an emergency refrigeration call was received at 2:30 P.M. on a Thursday. At 2:45 P.M. a message was left with service call to phone Harry's office. Harry is an appliance service technician. This day he had six calls to run and by 2:45 P.M. he had completed five and was headed for his last service call. At 3:45 P.M. Harry had not phoned in. A call to the customer's home revealed that Harry had left the place by 3:30 P.M. The manager and the head technician drove by Harry's home and found his service vehicle in his driveway at 3:55 P.M.

Next morning Harry was called into the manager's office where the head technician was also present. The manager and the head technician confronted Harry with "facts." Harry's dispatch claimed that the customer was "Not Home." He said that only a young girl was in the house, so he did not go in. This was acceptable to the manager and the head technician because it agreed with the company policy. Harry was asked if he understood a long standing company policy which required a technician to call the office upon completion of his assigned tasks and prior to returning to the office or going home. Harry said he had no reason not to call before going home.

The following Monday, Harry wanted to speak to the manager and the head technician. He said that he had been upset all weekend. He said that he had done an excellent job over his five years of employment. He resented being "followed" and accused the head technician of favoritism toward another service technician. He concluded by saying that he had worked through lunch, therefore his eight hours were completed by 4:00

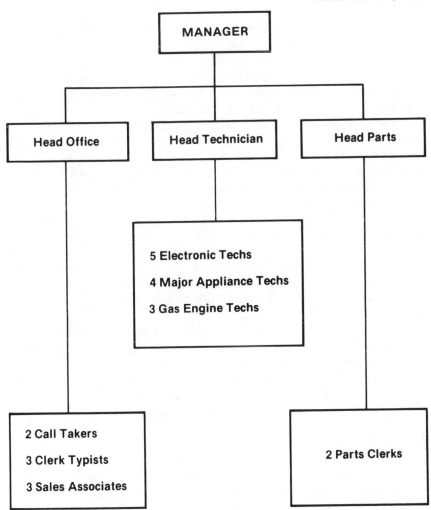

FIGURE A.1. Organization Structure of Minnis Service

P.M. The manager reminded Harry that he must have taken lunch by 1:00 P.M. according to labor laws and company bulletins, and that he went home prior to 4:00 P.M.

Harry claimed that a morale problem was developing among the techs and that regular meetings were needed to stop misunderstandings between the management and techs. The manager and head technician agreed with Harry's suggestion and told him that there would be a meeting on Friday. They also told Harry that they were reinstating the "call in policy" in an interhouse bulletin to all technicians.

The manager and Harry's co-workers think that Harry is a competent technician and maintains a high level of productivity. The manager decided not to take any action against Harry.

The manager and the head technician discussed Harry's comments and ulterior motives. They thought that Harry was attempting to make this incident look like a conflict between the management and technicians. However, no other technicians complained about poor morale or misunderstanding before. Harry was a known hothead during his five years with the company.

Harry's "Not at Home" customer had called the service unit and wanted to know when her "part" would be received. She stated that her neighbor went in her house with her daughter and the service technician. She further stated that the technician had gone down to the cellar, returned shortly, and said that he would have to order a part. He then left. The call was reassigned to Harry a day later and he repaired it with a part from his truck.

At the meeting on Friday, the "Call In" letter was distributed and explained. The technicians were told that the manager would like to discuss any problems in group meetings or in private, if preferred. Harry tried to make some comments on this, but the other technicians were not willing to engage in any disagreement. The management decided to ignore the situation and hoped that Harry would be satisfied.

Incident 2

Two months later, at the Friday meeting of the technicians, Harry had a hot exchange with another appliance technician. This was the technician that Harry had accused the head technician of favoring. The words between them got very personal. Both technicians blamed each other for technical incompetence and claimed the advantages of their own service area. At this point, another technician, Dick, joined Harry in attacking the other technician and quoted Harry's phraseology. The communication was allowed to run its course until the "favored" technician decided to leave and Harry was asked by the manager to tone down his voice. One of the appliance technicians observed that they worked as four independents which caused many of their problems. One of the electronics technicians stated that there was nothing wrong with the unit, "we just have two guys here who hate each other's guts!"

The meeting was brought to a conclusion when the manager said he would review the daily schedules of the appliance technicians for favoritism in assignments. He also promised to talk to each appliance technician individually over the next week. Information gained from the meetings with individual technicians indicated no concrete evidence of favoritism in assignments. Only Harry and Dick were related to these personnel problems. By this time, Dick apologized for verbally attacking his co-worker.

Incident 3

About three weeks later, the head office associate told the manager that she was questioned at the local store by the appliance and TV department manager about the "technical morale problem" at the service unit. The manager of this department is John Dickson who happens to be Harry's neighbor and golf partner. About two weeks after this, the previous service manager (now assigned to another state) disclosed that John Dickson had called and questioned him on the "decline of service" at service unit. During this period, a manager of another store told the manager (Minnis Service) that John was "gunning for him" and intended to review the service operation. This was definitely beyond any authority that John had, explicit or implicit.

The manager called Harry into his office and explained his disappointment. The manager told Harry that he should keep the service affairs within the unit and the unit should solve its own problems. The manager also observed that the involvement of the store in the internal affairs of service could undermine store-service relations which could not be tolerated.

It was reported that Harry and John were attempting to work-up service unit associates and store technicians. During the period of conflict, Harry has consistently adhered to company rules and procedures.

APPENDIX B

Exercises

In this section, eight exercises have been described which are designed for intervention in intrapersonal, interpersonal, intragroup, and intergroup organizational conflicts. These exercises have been designed for interventions in conflicts in ongoing organizations. They may be used in the classroom provided that appropriate changes in some instructions and time allocations to different steps are made.

The time allocated to different steps is based on estimates of the approximate time needed to perform each step. The allocation of time for each step may be changed depending on the nature of conflict involved, number of participants in an exercise, and time available for an exercise. Each exercise was tested in classrooms with undergraduate and MBA students and in workshops with managers. Therefore, changes in the design of the exercises should be avoided unless there are definite reasons for doing so.

The participants in the exercise should fill out the Rahim Organizational Conflict Inventory-I and II (ROCI-I and II) and prepare indices for different types of conflict and the styles of handling interpersonal conflict with superiors, subordinates, and peers.* The participants will require the help of the training staff in completing the inventories and preparing the indices.

The participants should read the eight chapters of this book after the inventories are completed but before beginning the exercises. The

---

*The *Rahim Organizational Conflict Inventory-I and II (Forms A, B, & C)* and the *Rahim Organizational Conflict Inventories: Professional Manual* are available from Consulting Psychologists Press, Inc., 577 College Avenue, Palo Alto, California 94306.

trainees may be assigned additional reading materials if the staff so desires. Appropriate movies may also be used to highlight some of the issues involved in a conflict and intervention strategies in managing conflict.

EXERCISE 1: CONTRACT BUILDING

OBJECTIVES

1. To help the participants know each other.
2. To assess the initial expectations, needs, and resources of the participants.
3. To provide a match between the expectations of the staff and participants in the conflict management workshops which are to follow.

PREMEETING PREPARATION

None.

REQUIREMENTS

1. Group size: Between 10 and 35.
2. Time required: 1 hour 15 minutes.
3. Materials: Felt pens, masking tapes, writing tablets, magic markers, and newsprints.
4. Physical arrangements: A large room with open space.

PROCEDURE

Step 1 (5 minutes)

1. The staff discusses the objectives of the exercise.
2. The staff presents the schedule for the exercise.
3. The staff entertains questions from the participants.

Step 2 (5 minutes)

The staff asks the participants to write down the following information on a sheet of paper from writing tablet:

1. Name
2. Expectations from the workshops.
3. Expertise, skills, or resources.

The participants may suggest additional items of information to be included in the list. The staff should also write down the above information on a sheet of paper.

Step 3 (35 minutes or less)

The participants and staff move around the room to examine and discuss each other's list.

Step 4 (15 minutes)

The staff invites comments from the participants regarding the following:

1. Is there any agreement among the participants as to what they expect from the workshops on conflict management which are to follow?
2. Are there any skills among the participants which can be used in the conflict management workshops?
3. Are there any concerns among the participants regarding the conflict workshops?

Step 5 (10 minutes)

1. The staff summarizes the expectations and concerns of the participants on newsprints.
2. The staff discusses whether and to what extent it is possible to satisfy the expectations of the participants.

Step 6 (5 minutes)

The staff asks the participants to make comments on this exercise.

EXERCISE 2: TECHNIQUE OF ROLE ANALYSIS

OBJECTIVES

1. To diagnose intrapersonal conflict.
2. To clarify the role of the focal role occupant.
3. To clarify the expectations of the focal role occupant from his group members.
4. To clarify the obligations of the focal role occupant to other members of his group.

PREMEETING PREPARATION

1. Complete the ROCI-I, to be supplied by the staff, and compute the index of your intrapersonal conflict with the help of the staff.
2. Read Chapters 1, 2, 3, and 4 of this book. Additional readings may be assigned by the staff.

REQUIREMENTS

1. Group size: Between 5 and 15.
2. Time required: 1 hour 52 minutes for each group member.
3. Materials: Felt pens, magic markers, writing tablets, masking tapes, and newsprints.
4. Physical arrangements: A room with chairs which can be easily rearranged.

PROCEDURE

Step 1 (5 minutes)

1. The leader of the participating group or staff explains the objectives of the exercise.
2. The group leader and/or the staff entertains questions from the participants.

Step 2 (15 minutes)

1. The staff presents the results of the analysis of data collected on the ROCI-I. Additional data that the staff may have collected by interviewing the group members should also be presented.
2. The staff and participants discuss the results and draw inferences.
3. The staff presents the schedule for the exercise.

Step 3 (5 minutes)

The focal role occupant initiates discussion regarding his role and how it matches with the goals of the group.

Step 4 (30 minutes)

1. The focal role occupant lists the activities that he feels occupy his role on the newsprints.

2. The group members discuss these activities so that new items are added and ambiguous or contradictory items dropped.

Step 5 (30 minutes)

1. The focal role occupant lists his expectations form his group members.
2. The group members discuss these expectations to revise and clarify the list and accept their obligations.

Step 6 (20 minutes)

1. Each group member presents his list of expectations from the focal role occupant.
2. This list is discussed and revised until it is agreed upon by the group.

Step 7 (2 minutes)

1. The staff asks the focal role occupant to write down the role profile consisting of (a) prescribed and discretionary activities of the focal role occupant, (b) expectations of the focal role occupant from other roles in the group, and (c) obligation of this (his) role to other roles in the group.
2. A copy of this role profile is distributed to each participant before the next meeting.

Step 8 (5 minutes)

The staff asks the participants to make comments on the exercise and the new behavior they learned from it.

Steps 3 through 7 are repeated for each of the remaining members of the group.

EXERCISE 3: JOB DESIGN

OBJECTIVES

1. To diagnose intrapersonal conflict.
2. To prepare a list of changes that are needed to redesign a specific job.

PREMEETING PREPARATION

1. The organizational members whose jobs are to be redesigned respond to the ROCI-I, supplied by the staff, and construct the index of intrapersonal conflict, with the help of the staff.
2. Read chapters 1, 2, 3, and 4 of this book. Additional readings may be assigned by the staff.

The above two steps are not needed if the participants have already done these for Exercise 2.

REQUIREMENTS

1. Group size: Between 5 and 25.
2. Time required: 1 hour and 35 minutes.
3. Materials: Felt pens, magic markers, writing tablets, masking tapes, and newsprints.
4. Physical arrangements: A large room with chairs which can be easily rearranged.

PROCEDURE

Step 1 (5 minutes)

1. The group leader or staff discusses the objectives of the meeting.
2. The group leader or staff announces the job which has to be redesigned.
3. The staff presents the schedule for the exercise.
4. The staff entertains questions from the participants.

Step 2 (15 minutes)

1. The staff presents the results of the analysis of data collected on the ROCI-I. Additional data that the staff may have collected by interviewing the group members should also be presented.
2. The staff and participants discuss the results and draw inferences.

The above two steps must be excluded if these were done for Exercise 2.

Step 3 (30 minutes)

1. Break into subgroups of 5 and 6 and elect your respective leaders to discuss how the job, assigned to you, in Step 1 can be redesigned.
2. Brainstorm a list of changes that are needed to redesign the job. In preparing the list, consider how the job can be redesigned to increase its skill variety, task identity, task significance, autonomy, and feedback, as explained in Chapter 4.
3. List the changes recommended by your subgroup on newsprints.

Step 4 (30 minutes)

A fishbowl exercise may be arranged for this purpose.

1. Post the newsprint listings of changes recommended by subgroups on the walls.
2. The subgroup leaders present the list of changes, recommended by their subgroups, to the group.
3. The group discusses the changes and prepares the final list of changes that are to be made in the redesigned job. The list is appropriately screened for ambiguous and redundant items.

Step 5 (10 minutes)

1. The group assigns responsibilities for implementation of changes in job design and monitoring of implementation to specified individuals.
2. A date is agreed for follow-up.

Step 6 (5 minutes)

The staff asks the participants to make comments on the exercise and the new behavior they learned from it.

EXERCISE 4: TRANSACTIONAL ANALYSIS

OBJECTIVES

1. To diagnose the styles of handling interpersonal conflict with superior(s), subordinates, and peers.

2. To enhance the awareness of the positions of superior(s), subordinates, and peers.
3. To enhance authentic communication with a person's superior(s), subordinates, and peers.

PREMEETING PREPARATION

1. Complete the ROCI-II (Forms A, B, and C), to be supplied by the staff, and construct the indices of your styles of handling interpersonal conflict with superior(s), subordinates, and peers, with the help of the staff.
2. Read Chapter 5 of this book. Additional readings may be assigned by the staff.
3. Write the parent, adult, and child responses to the five statements in Step 4 (1) on your writing tablet.

REQUIREMENTS

1. Group size: Between 6 and 30.
2. Time required: 1 hour and 48 minutes.
3. Materials: Felt pens and writing tablets.
4. Physical arrangement: A large room where the trios can have private discussions. The room should have chairs which can be easily rearranged.

PROCEDURES

Step 1 (5 minutes)

1. The group leader or staff discusses the objectives of the meeting.
2. The staff presents the schedule for the meeting.
3. The staff entertains questions from the participants.

Step 2 (30 minutes)

1. The staff presents the results of analysis of data collected on the ROCI-II. Additional data (especially on the effective use of the five styles of handling interpersonal conflict) that the staff may have collected through observation and interviews of group members may also be presented.
2. The staff and participants discuss the results and draw inferences.

Step 3 (2 minutes)

Break into subgroups of three members. You should choose members with whom you will be able to discuss your work-related problems openly.

Step 4 (25 minutes)

1. Write a parent, adult, and child response to the following five statements: [The participants have done this before coming to the workshop.]

   a. Did you see the sales figures for this month?
   b. I have to finish this report today.
   c. What time is it?
   d. Jim, you are late.
   e. My boss is a competent person.

2. Discuss your responses to the above statements with your group members.
3. Write a group response (parent, adult, and child) for each of the five statements.

Step 5 (6 minutes)

Think of a work incident that occurred between you and your boss. Quickly relate the story to the other members. Agree upon which of the three stories would make the best role-playing exercise.

The individual to whom the incident occurred is designated as member A who becomes the observer. The other two are designated B and C.

Step 6 (5 minutes)

Member B: Assume you are the boss in the situation described by member A. Start at the beginning and role-play it through to conclusion. Play the role according to how you would feel and behave if you were in the situation. Make up what is consistent with the story when you need to do so.

---

*Steps 5 through 8 of this exercise are based on an exercise developed by M.D. Federer, Department of Psychology, California Polytechnic State University, San Luis, Obispo, California.

Member C: Assume you are the subordinate and follow the same role-playing instructions.

Member A: While observing, do not interrupt the role-playing. Watch for the following:

1. Primary ego states from which each is communicating.
2. Changes in ego states as the exercise progresses.
3. Complementary, crossed, and ulterior transactions.

Step 7 (15 minutes)

1. Member A describes his observations on role-playing to members B and C.
2. The triad members discuss the following:
   a. What did each of the role players try to accomplish?
   b. How would you characterize the final solution(s) arrived at by members B and C? Starting with the ego state of the boss, would you say the transaction was (a) Parent to Child, (b) Child to Parent, (c) Adult to Adult, or (d) Child to Child?
   c. How did the subordinate feel about the transactions?
   d. What would appear to be possible consequences of the transactions?
   e. How could the situation have best been handled in terms of (a) type of communication, (b) specific approaches to overcome conflict, (c) solutions?

Step 8 (10 minutes)

Member A's are to report some of their observations to the total

Step 9 (10 minutes)

The staff asks the participants to make comments on the exercise and the new behavior learned from it.

EXERCISE 5: TEAM BUILDING

OBJECTIVES

1. To diagnose intragroup conflict.
2. To reach consensus on the goals of the group. This may involve adding new goals and dropping, or redefining existing goals.
3. To analyze the tasks that are performed to attain the group's goals. This may involve adding new tasks and dropping, or redefining existing tasks to attain the revised goals.

4. To assign or reassign the tasks to the group members.
5. To examine the group processes and the interpersonal relationships among the group members.

REQUIREMENTS

1. Group size: 6 to 40.
2. Time: 7 hours 45 minutes.
3. Materials: Felt pens, magic markers, writing tablets, masking tapes, and newsprints.
4. Physical arrangements: A large room with chairs which can be easily rearranged.

PREMEETING PREPARATION

1. Complete the ROCI-I and ROCI-II (Form C), to be supplied by the staff, and construct indices of the amount of conflict in your group and your styles of handling conflict with your group members. The phrasing of the items in the ROCI-I and ROCI-II must be altered to make the information useful to the group members.
2. Read chapter 6 of this book. Additional readings may be assigned by the staff.

PROCEDURES

Step 1 (5 minutes)

1. The group leader or staff explains the objectives of the meeting.
2. The staff presents the schedule for the meeting.
3. The group leader and/or the staff entertains questions from the participants.

Step 2 (20 minutes)

1. The staff presents the findings of conflict diagnosis performed on the group members through the ROCI-I and ROCI-II. The staff also discusses the summary of data collected from group members through observations and interviews.
2. The staff and participants discuss the results of data analysis and draw inferences.

Step 3 (45 minutes)

1. Break into subgroups of 5 or 6 members to evaluate the existing goals of the group to prepare a revised list of goals.
2. Elect a leader for your subgroup.
3. List the revised goals of your group on the newsprint.

Step 4 (45 minutes)

A fishbowl exercise may be arranged for this step.

1. Post the newsprint listing of the revised group goals on the walls.
2. The subgroup leaders present the goals identified by their subgroups to the group.
3. The group prepares the final list of goals.

Step 5 (10 minutes)

The subgroup leaders rank the final list of goals in importance with the help of group members.

Step 6 (60 minutes)

1. Break into subgroups of 5 or 6 members to prepare a list of tasks which must be performed to attain the goals agreed upon in Step 4.
2. Assign each subgroup to work on the tasks for one or two group goals prepared in Step 4.
3. Elect your subgroup leader.
4. List the tasks needed to attain the group goals assigned to you on newsprints.

Step 7 (60 minutes)

A fishbowl exercise may be arranged for this purpose.

1. Post the newsprint listing of the tasks on the walls.
2. The subgroup leaders present the tasks identified by their subgroups to the group.
3. The group discusses and integrates the tasks identified by the subgroups.
4. The group prepares the final list of tasks that are needed to attain the revised goals.

Step 8 (30 minutes)

1. The group leader, with the help of subgroup leaders, assigns responsibilities for different tasks to group members.
2. The interdependent activities among group members are discussed and clarified. Some individuals may be made specifically responsible for the management of interface activities between units within the group.

Step 9 (45 minutes)

1. Break into subgroups of 5 or 6.
2. Elect your subgroup leader.
3. Discuss the problems which are hindering the attainment of group goals. The subgroup members may like to discuss the group processes, such as leadership, decision-making, communication, and motivation processes, and interpersonal issues, such as styles of handling conflict, trust, support, etc.
4. Prepare separate listings of group processes and interpersonal issues on newsprints.

Step 10 (45 minutes)

A fishbowl exercise may be arranged for this purpose.

1. Post the newsprint listings of group processes and interpersonal relations from the subgroups on the walls.
2. The subgroup leaders present the problems relating to group processes and interpersonal issues.
3. The group members discuss these problems and prepare a final list of problems, which should be properly dealt with, to improve group effectiveness.
4. The participants rank the problems in order of importance.
5. Each subgroup is made responsible for formulating solutions to one or more specific problems identified in Step 10 (3).

Step 11 (30 minutes)

1. Join your subgroup to discuss the problem(s) assigned to your subgroup.
2. Elect your subgroup leader.
3. Prepare alternative solutions to the problem(s).
4. List the solutions to problems on newsprint.

Step 12 (45 minutes)

1. Post the newsprint listing of problem solutions on the walls.
2. The subgroup leaders present the alternative solutions to their assigned problems.
3. The group members discuss these solutions and reach agreement on the solutions.

Step 13 (10 minutes)

1. The participants elect three or more members for developing strategies needed for the implementation of changes recommended by the group. The group members can indicate several broad strategies for the implementation of changes.
2. The members are made responsible for securing approval for changes from the formal leader of the group. (On receiving the approval, they prepare the strategies for implementation and follow these for making the planned changes.)
3. Dates for follow-up are agreed upon.

Step 14 (15 minutes)

The staff asks the participants to make comments on the exercise and the new behavior that they learned which can be used in their group.

EXERCISE 6: INTERGROUP PROBLEM SOLVING

OBJECTIVES

1. To diagnose the amount of conflict between two specific groups and how it is handled.
2. To help the participants identify intergroup problems.
3. To help the participants develop alternative solutions to these problems.
4. To design plans for implementation of intergroup decisions.
5. To help ingroup members learn the intergrating style of handling conflict with outgroup members.

REQUIREMENTS

1. Group size: Between 15 and 35.
2. Time required: 6 hours 15 minutes for the first session and 2 hours 35 minutes for the second session.

3. Materials: Felt pens, magic markers, writing tablets, masking tapes, and newsprints.
4. Physical arrangement: One large room and several smaller rooms with chairs which can be easily rearranged.

ADVANCE PREPARATION

1. Complete the ROCI-I and ROCI-II (Form C) to be supplied by the staff, and construct indices of the amount of conflict between the two groups and the styles of handling such conflict by the members of the two groups, with the help of the staff. The items of the instruments must be altered to make the information useful to the two conflicting groups.
2. Read Chapter 7 of this book. The staff may assign additional readings.

Step 1 (5 minutes)

1. The leaders of the two groups or staff present the objectives of the of the exercise.
2. The staff presents the schedule for the exercise.
3. The leaders of the participating groups and/or staff entertain questions from the participants.

Step 2 (10 minutes)

1. The staff presents the five major steps in problem solving.
2. The staff entertains questions from the participants.

Step 3 (30 minutes)

1. The staff presents the results of the analysis of data collected on the ROCIs. The staff also presents the summary of additional data that may have been collected from the members of the participating groups.
2. The staff and participants discuss the results and draw inferences.

Step 4 (45 minutes)

1. Break into homogeneous subgroups and meet separately to discuss and identify the intergroup problems.

2. Elect your subgroup leader.
3. List the intergroup problems on newsprint.

Step 5 (45 minutes)

A fishbowl exercise may be arranged for this step.

1. Post the newsprint listings of intergroup problems on the walls.
2. The subgroup leaders present the problems identified by their subgroups to the intergroup.
3. The intergroup discusses and intergrates the problems identified by the subgroups. It prepares the final list of problems.

Step 6 (10 minutes)

1. The subgroup leaders rank the final list of problems.
2. Each subgroup is assigned to work on the solutions of one or more specific problems.

Step 7 (15 minutes)

The intergroup formulates criteria for solutions.

Step 8 (30 minutes)

1. Break into heterogeneous subgroups and meet separately to discuss and formulate alternative solutions to problems assigned to your subgroup with reference to Step 7.
2. Elect your subgroup leader.
3. List the alternative solutions to problems on the newsprints.

Step 9 (45 minutes)

A fishbowl exercise may be arranged for this purpose.

1. Post the newsprint listings of alternative solutions on the walls.
2. The subgroup leaders discuss the alternative solutions to their assigned problems.
3. The intergroup discusses and integrates the alternative solutions.
4. The subgroup leaders rank the alternative solutions to each problem.

Step 10 (30 minutes)

The subgroups created in Step 8 prepare a plan for implementation (including monitoring of implementation) of the problem solutions.

Step 11 (45 minutes)

A fishbowl exercise may be arranged for this step.

1. The subgroup leaders present the plans prepared by their respective subgroups.
2. The subgroup leaders prepare the final plan for implementation.

Step 12 (45 minutes)

1. The subgroup leaders, with the help of participants, identify the problem of implementation.
2. They prepare strategies for overcoming resistance to change. A force field analysis may be performed for this purpose.

Step 13 (5 minutes)

The intergroup assigns responsibilities for implementation and monitoring of implementation to specified individuals.

Step 14 (5 minutes)

The intergroup prepares a schedule for follow-up.

Step 15 (10 minutes)

The staff asks the participants to make comments on the exercise and the new behavior learned from it.
[The first problem-solving session concludes here.]

Second Problem-Solving Session

The objective of this session is to evaluate the impact of implementation of the plan as specified in Step 11 in the previous session and recommend corrective measures.

Step 1 (5 minutes)

1. The leaders of the participating groups or the staff present the objectives of the second session for problem solving.
2. The staff presents a schedule for the exercise.
3. They entertain questions from the participants.

Step 2 (30 minutes)

A fishbowl exercise may be arranged for this step.

The individuals who were responsible for the implementation and monitoring of implementation discuss the progess made in implementation and problems encountered.

Step 3 (45 minutes)

The intergroup discusses the impact of the plan and identifies the problems of implementation, if any.

Step 4 (15 minutes)

The intergroup may recommend corrective actions if the results of implementation deviate from the standards.

Step 5 (45 minutes)

1. The participants may respond to the ROCI-I and ROCI-II. They compute indices of the amount of conflict between the two groups and their styles of handling such conflict.
2. The conflict indices from the first session are compared with corresponding indices from the second session.
3. The staff and the participants discuss the changes in the amount of conflict and styles of handling interpersonal conflict between the two sessions and draw inferences.

Step 6 (10 minutes)

The intergroup decided whether or not to recycle the problem-solving process.

Step 7 (5 minutes)

The staff asks the participants to make comments on the exercise and the new behavior learnt from it.

EXERCISE 7: ORGANIZATIONAL MIRRORING

OBJECTIVES

1. To improve relationships among three or more groups.
2. To receive feedback from the work-related groups.

PREMEETING PREPARATION

Read Chapter 7 of this book if you have not done it already. The staff may assign additional readings.

REQUIREMENTS

1. Group size: Between 30 and 80.
2. Time required: 5 hours 20 minutes.
3. Materials: Felt pens, magic markers, writing tablets, masking tapes, and newsprints.
4. Physical arrangements: A large room with chairs which can be easily rearranged.

PROCEDURE

Step 1 (10 minutes)

1. The leaders of the participating groups and/or the staff explain the objectives of the exercise.
2. The staff presents the schedule for the exercise.
3. The leaders of the participating groups and the staff entertain questions from the participants.

Step 2 (30 minutes)

1. The staff presents the findings of the conflict diagnosis performed on the participating groups through interview and other methods.

2. The staff and the participants discuss the results of diagnosis and draw inferences.

Step 3 (60 minutes)

1. The members of work-related groups form a "fishbowl" to interpret and discuss the data presented by the consultant.
2. The host group members listen and take notes.

Step 4 (60 minutes)

The host group members form a "fishbowl" to discuss what they learned from work-related groups. They may ask for clarification from the leaders of work-related groups.

Step 5 (30 minutes)

1. Break into heterogeneous subgroups to identify the significant intergroup problems which must be solved to enhance the host group's effectiveness.
2. Elect leader for your subgroup.
3. List the problems on newsprint.

Step 6 (45 minutes)

A fishbowl exercise may be performed for this step.

1. Post the newsprint listings of problems on the walls.
2. The subgroup leaders report the problems identified by their respective subgroups.
3. The subgroup leaders discuss these problems and prepare a final list for which actions are needed.
4. Each subgroup is made responsible to formulate the solutions of one or more problems.

Step 7 (45 minutes)

1. The subgroups formed before discuss their assigned problem(s) and formulate alternative solutions.
2. The subgroups prepare action plans and strategies for implementation for the solutions in the previous step.

Step 8 (30 minutes)

1. The leaders of the subgroups review and accept the action plans
   and strategies of implementation.
2. A schedule for follow-up is agreed upon.

Step 9 (10 minutes)

The staff asks the participants to make comments on the exercise
and the new behavior learned from it.

EXERCISE 8: ANALYSIS OF TASK INTERDEPENDENCE

OBJECTIVES

1. To analyze the interrelationships of tasks between the participating groups.
2. To prepare a list of interdependent task items and classify them
   into homogeneous clusters.
3. To assign the task clusters to groups and an integrative committee.

REQUIREMENTS

1. Group size: 15 to 35.
2. Time required: 3 hours and 55 minutes.
3. Materials: Felt pens, magic markers, writing tablets, masking
   tapes, newsprints.
4. Physical arangement: A large room with chairs which can be
   easily rearranged.

PREMEETING PREPARATION

Read Chapter 7 of this book if you have not done it already. The staff
may assign additional readings.

Step 1 (10 minutes)

1. The leaders of the participating groups and/or staff discuss the
   objectives of the meeting.
2. The staff presents the schedule for the exercise.

3. The leaders of the participating groups and the staff entertain questions from the participants.

Step 2 (15 minutes)

1. The staff presents results of the analysis of diagnostic data which may have been collected from the participating groups.
2. The staff and participants discuss the results and draw inferences.

Step 3 (60 minutes)

1. Break into heterogeneous subgroups to identify the task items which create problems between the participating groups.
2. Elect a leader for your subgroup.
3. On newsprint, list the task items which create intergroup problems.

Step 4 (60 minutes)

A fishbowl exercise may be arranged for this step.

1. The subgroup leaders present the tasks identified by their subgroups to the intergroup.
2. The intergroup discusses and integrates the tasks identified by the subgroups. The intergroup prepares the final list of tasks.

Step 5 (45 minutes)

1. The subgroup leaders classify the tasks into several clusters on the basis of similarity of task items.
2. They assign a short title to each task cluster.

Step 6 (30 minutes)

1. The formal group leaders, with the help of subgroup leaders, assign the task clusters to participating groups. The task clusters must be assigned to the groups on the basis of congruence between the requirements of the tasks and skill, material, and other resources possessed by the groups for performing the tasks.

2. The task clusters which cannot be assigned to a particular group because no group has the expertise, resources, or authority to perform the tasks in these clusters should be assigned to a special committee formed for this purpose with three or more members from the participating groups.

Step 7 (5 minutes)

1. A special committee is made responsible for the supervision of implementation of changes agreed by the intergroup.
2. A date(s) for follow-up is agreed upon.

Step 8 (10 minutes)

The staff asks the participants to make comments on the exercise and the new behavior they learnt from the execise.

Bibliography

Abell, P. (1975). *Organizations as bargaining and influence systems.* New York: Halsted.

Albeda, W. (1977). Between harmony and conflict: Industrial democracy in the Netherlands. *The Annals of the American Academy of Political and Social Science, 431*(5), 74-82.

Aldrich, H. (1971). Organizational boundaries and inter-organizational conflict. *Human Relations, 24,* 279-293.

Arnold, J. D. (1978). *Make up your mind: The seven building blocks to better decisions.* New York: AMACOM.

Assael, H. (1968). The political role of trade associations in distributive conflict resolution. *Journal of Marketing, 32*(4), 21-28.

Axelrod, R. (1970). *Conflict of interest: A theory of divergent goals with applications to politics.* Chicago: Markham.

Axelsson, R., & Rosenberg, L. (1979). Decision-making and organizational turbulence. *Acta Sociologica, 22,* 45-62.

Bach, G. R., & Wyden, P. (1968). *The intimate enemy: How to fight fair in love and marriage.* New York: Avon Books.

Barbash, J. (1980). Collective bargaining and the theory of conflict. *British Journal of Industrial Relations, 17,* 82-90.

Baron, R. A. (1984). Reducing organizational conflict: An incompatible response approach. *Journal of Applied Psychology, 69,* 272-279.

Barton, A. H. (1975). Consensus and conflict among American leaders. *Public Opinion Quarterly, 38,* 507-530.

Batlis, N. C. (1980). Dimensions of role conflict and relationships with individual outcomes. *Peceptual and Motor Skills, 51,* 179-185.

Baumgarter, T., Buckley, W., & Burns, T. (1975). Relational control: The human structuring of cooperation and conflict. *Journal of Conflict Resolution, 19,* 417-440.

Bazerman, M. H., & Neale, M. A. (1982). Improving negotiation effectiveness under final offer arbitration: The role of selection and training. *Journal of Applied Psychology, 67,* 543-548.

Beck, E. M., & Betz, M. (1975). A comparative analysis of organizational conflict in schools. *Sociology of Education, 48,* 59-74.

Bedeian, A. G., & Armenakis, A. A. (1981). A path-analytic study of the consequences of role conflict and ambiguity. *Academy of Management Journal, 24,* 417-424.

Benjamin, A. J., & Levi, A. M. (1979). Process minefields in intergroup conflict resolution: The Sdot Yam workshop. *Journal of Applied Behavioral Science, 15,* 507-520.

Bernardin, J. H., & Alvares, K. M. (1975). The effects of organizational level on perceptions of role conflict resolution strategy. *Organizational Behavior and Human Performance, 14,*1-9.

Bernardin, H. J., & Alvares, K. M. (1976). The managerial grid as a predictor of conflict resolution method and managerial effectiveness. *Administrative Science Quarterly, 21,* 84-92.

Bigoness, W. J. (1976). Effects of locus of control and style of third party intervention upon bargaining behavior. *Journal of Applied Psychology, 16,* 305-312.

Bigoness, W. J. (1983). Distributive versus integrative approaches to negotiation: Experiential through learning a negotiation simulation. *Developments in Business Simulation & Experiential Learning,* 64-67.

Blake, R. P., & Mouton, J. S. (1961). Comprehension of own and outgroup positions under intergroup competition. *Journal of Conflict Resolution, 5,* 304-310.

Blake, R. R., & Mouton, J. S. (1984). Overcoming group warfare: How should you go about reconciling the differences between groups that need to cooperate but that already have swords drawn? *Harvard Business Review, 62*(6), 98-108.

Blerkom, M. V., & Tjosvold, D. (1981). Effects of social context and other's competence on engaging in controversy. *Journal of Social Psychology, 107,* 141-145.

Bomers, G. B. J., & Peterson, R. B. (Eds.). (1982). *Conflict management and industrial relations.* Boston: Kluwer-Nijhoff.

Bondurant, J. V., & Fisher, M. W. (Eds.). (1971). *Conflict: Violence and nonviolence.* New York: Aldine-Atherton.

Bonoma, T. V. (1976). Conflict, cooperation and trust in three power systems. *Behavioral Science, 21,* 499-514.

Boulding, K. E. (1957). Organization and conflict. *Journal of Conflict Resolution, 1,* 122-134.

Boulding, K. E. (1973). Equality and conflict. *The Annals of the American Academy of Political and Social Science,* 409 (9), 1-8.

Brehmer, B. (1976). Social judgment theory and the analysis of interpersonal conflict. *Psychological Bulletin, 83,* 985-1003.

Brehmer, B., & Hammond, K. R. (1973). Cognitive sources of interpersonal conflict: Analysis of interactions between linear and nonlinear cognitive systems. *Organizational Behavior and Human Performance, 10,* 290-313.

Brown, C. T., Yelsma, P., & Keller, P. W. (1981). Communication-conflict predisposition: Development of a theory and an instrument. *Human Relation, 34,* 1103-1117.

Brown, J. S. (1957). Principles of intrapersonal conflict. *Journal of Conflict Resolution, 1,* 135-154.

Brown, L. D. (1977). Can "Haves" and "Have-Nots" cooperate? Two efforts to bridge a social gap. *Journal of Applied Behavioral Science, 13,* 211-224.

Brown, L. D. (1978). Toward a theory of power and intergroup relations. In C. L. Cooper & C. P. Alderfer (Eds.), *Advances in experiential social process* (Vol. 1, pp. 161-180). New York: Wiley.

Brown, L. D. (1979). Managing conflict among groups. In D. A. Kolb, I. M. Rubin, & J.M. MacIntryre (Eds.), *Organizational psychology: A book of readings* (3rd ed., pp. 377-389). Englewood Cliffs, N.J.: Prentice-Hall.

Burton, J. W. (1969). *Conflict and communication.* London: Macmillan.

Butler, A. G., Jr. (1973). Project management: A study in organizational conflict. *Academy of Management Journal, 16,* 84-101.

Butler, A. S., & Maher, C. A. (1981). Conflict and special service teams: Perspectives and suggestions for school psychologists. *Journal of School Psychology, 19,* 62-70.

Byrnes, J. F. (in press). *Conflict resolution.* New York: American Management Association.

Cafferty, T. P., & Streufert, S. (1974). Conflict and attitudes toward the opponent: An application of the Collins and Hoyt attitude change theory to groups in interorganizational conflict. *Journal of Applied Psychology, 59,* 48-53.

Chesler, M. A., Crowfoot, J. E., & Bryant, B. I. (1978). Power training: An alternative path to conflict management. *California Management Review, 21*(2), 84-90.

Cochran, D. S., Schnake, M., & Earl, R. (1983). Effect of organizational size on conflict frequency and location in hospitals. *Journal of Management Studies, 20,* 441-451.

Cochran, D. S., & White, D. D. (1981). Intraorganizational conflict in the hospital purchasing decision making process. *Academy of Management Journal, 24,* 324-332.

Cole, D. W. (Ed.). (1983). *Conflict resolution technology.* Cleveland: Organization Development Institute.

Collins, R. A. (1975). *Conflict sociology: Toward an explanatory science.* New York: Academic Press.

Coser, L. A. (1961). The termination of conflict. *Journal of Conflict Resolution, 5,* 347-353.

Cosier, R. A., & Ruble, T. L. (1981). Research on conflict-handling behavior: An experimental approach. *Academy of Management Journal, 24,* 816-831.

Cosier, R. A. (1982). Methods of improving the strategic decision: Dialectic versus the devil's advocate. *Strategic Management Journal, 3,* 373-374.

Dahrendorf, R. (1958). Toward a theory of social conflict. *Journal of Conflict Resolution, 2,* 170-183.

Dando, M. R., & Bee, A. J. (1977). Operational research for complex conflicts: A gaming methodology for the development of a decision-making. *Operational Research Quarterly, 28,* 853-864.

Darkenwald, G. G., Jr. (1971). Organizational conflict in colleges and universities. *Administrative Science Quarterly, 16*, 407–412.

Derr, C. B. (1972). Conflict resolution in organizations: Views from the field of educational administration. *Public Administration Review, 32*, 495–501.

Derr, C. B. (1978). Managing organizational conflict: Collaboration, bargaining, and power approaches. *California Management Review, 21*(2), 76–83.

Deutsch, M. (1971). Toward an understanding of conflict. *International Journal of Group Tensions, 1*, 42–54.

Deutsch, M. (1973). *The resolution of conflict: Constructive and destructive process.* New Haven, CT.: Yale University Press.

Deutsch, M. (1980). Fifty years of conflict. In Festinger, L. (Ed.), *Retrospections on social psychology* (pp. 46–77, 259–265). New York: Oxford University Press.

Doob, L. W. (Ed.). (1970). *Resolving conflict in Africa: The Fermeda workshop.* New Haven, CT.: Yale University Press.

Doob, L. W. (1974). A Cyprus workshop: An exercise in intervention methodology. *Journal of Social Psychology, 94*, 161–174.

Druckman, D. (1971). The influence of the situation in interparty conflict. *Journal of Conflict Resolution, 15*, 523–554.

Duke, J. T. (1976). *Conflict and power in social life.* Provo, UT.: Brigham Young University Press.

Dutton, J. M., & Walton, R. E. (1966). Interdepartmental conflict and cooperation: Two contrasting studies. *Human Organization, 25*, 207–220.

Eiseman, J. W. (1977). A third-party consultation model for resolving recurring conflicts collaboratively. *Journal of Applied Behavioral Science, 13*, 303–314.

Eiseman, J. W. (1978). Reconciling "incompatible" positions. *Journal of Applied Behavioral Science, 14*, 133–150.

Ellis, D., & Fisher, B. A. (1975). Phases of conflict in small group development: A Markov analysis. *Human Communication Research, 1*, 195–212.

Ephron, L. R. (1961). Group conflict in organizations: A critical appraisal of recent theories. *Berkeley Journal of Sociology, 6*, 53–72.

Etzioni-Halevy, E. (1975). Patterns of conflict generation and conflict "absorption." *Journal of Conflict Resolution, 19*, 286–309.

Evan, W. M., & MacDougall, J. A. (1967). Interorganizational conflict: A labor-management bargaining experiment. *Journal of Conflict Resolution, 11*, 398–413.

Ewing, D. W. (1964). Tension can be an asset. *Harvard Business Review, 42*(5), 71–78.

Filley, A. C. (1977). Conflict resolution: The ethnic of the good loser. In R. C. Huseman, C. M. Logue, & D. L. Freshly (Eds.), *Readings in interpersonal and organizational behavior.* Boston: Holbrook.

Filley, A. C. (1978). Some normative issues in conflict management. *California Management Review, 20*(2), 61–66.

Fink, C. F. (1972). Conflict management strategies implied by expected utility models of behavior. *American Behavioral Scientist, 15*, 837–858.

Fisher, R. J.(1983). Third party consultation as a method of intergroup conflict resolution: A review studies. *Journal of Conflict Resolution, 27*, 301–344.

Ford, N. M., Walker, O. C., & Churchill, G. A., Jr. (1975). Expectation-specific measures of the intersender conflict and role ambiguity experienced by industrial salesman. *Journal of Business Research, 3*, 95–112.

Gill, C. G., & Warner, M. (1979). Managerial and organizational determinants of industrial conflict: The chemical industry case. *Journal of Management Studies, 16*, 56–59.

Goodge, P. (1978). Intergroup conflict: A rethink. *Human Relations, 31*, 475–487.

Gray-Little, B. (1974). Attitudes toward conflict with authority as a function of sex, I-E, and dogmatism. *Psychological Reports, 34*, 375–381.

Gricar, B. G., & Brown, L. D. (1981). Conflict, power, and organization in a changing community. *Human Relations, 34*, 877–893.

Gustafson, J. P., Cooper, L., Lathrop, N. C., Ringler, K., Seldin, F. A., & Wright, M. K. (1981). Cooperative and clashing interests in small groups. Part I: Theory. *Human Relations, 34*, 315-339.

Gustafson, J. P., Cooper, L., Lathrop, N. C., Ringler, K., Seldin, F. A., & Wright, M. K. (1981). Cooperative and clashing interests in small groups. Part II: Group narratives. *Human Relations, 34*, 367–378.

Hacon, R. J. (1964). *Conflict and human relations training.* New York: Pergamon Press.

Hagan, J., Gillis, A. R., & Chan, J. (1978). Explaining official delinquency: A spatial study of class, conflict and control. *Sociological Quarterly, 19*, 386-398.

Hall, D. T. (1972). A model of coping with role conflict: The role behavior of college educated women. *Administrative Science Quarterly, 17*, 471–486.

Hall, D. T., & Gordon, F. E. (1973). Career choices of married women: Effects of conflict, role behavior and satisfaction. *Journal of Applied Psychology, 58*, 42–48.

Hammond, K. R. (1965). New directions in research on conflict resolution. *Journal of Social Issues, 21*, 44–66.

Hammond, K. R., Todd, F. J., Wilkins, M., & Mitchell, T. O. (1966). Cognitive conflict between persons: Applications of the "Lens model" paradigm. *Journal of Experimental Social Psychology, 2*, 343-360.

Hanes. L. D., & Smith, D. (1973). A critique of assumptions underlying the study of communication in conflict. *Quarterly Journal of Speech, 59*, 423–435.

Harary, F., & Batell, M. F. (1981). Communication conflict. *Human Relations, 34*, 633–641.

Harnett, D. L., Cummings, L. L., & Hamner, W. C. (1973). Personality, bargaining style and payoff in bilateral monopoly bargaining among European managers. *Sociometry, 36*, 325-345.

Harnett, D. L., & Cummings, L. L. (1980). *Bargaining behavior: An international study.* Houston: Dame.

Harrison, R. (1972). Understanding your organization's character. *Harvard Business Review, 50* (3), 119-128.

Hartman, E. A., Phillips, J. L., & Cole S. G. (1976). Conflict and survival in triads. *Journal of Conflict Resolution, 20*, 589-607.

Hawes, L. C., & Smith, D. H. (1963). A critique of assumptions underlying the study of communication in conflict. *Quarterly Journal of Speech, 59*, 423-435.

Heckathorn, D. (1980). A unified model for bargaining and conflict. *Behavioral Science, 25*, 261–284.

Heichberger, R. L. (1974). A theoretical approach to conflict in organizational change processes. *Education, 94*, 205–236.

Henderson, B. D. (1967). Brinkmanship in business. *Harvard Business Review, 45* (2), 49–55.

Henderson, H. (1971). Toward managing social conflict. *Harvard Business Review, 49* (3), 82–90.

Hibbs, D. A., Jr. (1976). Industrial conflict in advanced industrial societies. *American Political Science Review, 70*, 1033–1058.

Hill, R. E. (1977). Managing interpersonal conflict in project teams. *Sloan Management Review, 18*(2), 45–61.

Himes, J. S. (1980). *Conflict and conflict management*. Athens: University of Georgia Press.

Hirshleifer, J. (1978). Competition, cooperation, and conflict in economics and biology. *Economics and Biology, 68*, 238–243.

Hocker-Wilmot, J., & Wilmot, W. W. (1978). *Interpersonal conflict*. Dubuque, IA: Wm. C. Brown.

Hottes, J. H., & Kahn, A. (1974). Sex differences in a mixed-motive conflict situation. *Journal of Personality, 42*, 260–275.

Jackson, J. (1975). Normative power and conflict potential. *Sociological Methods and Research, 4*, 237–263.

Jandt. F. E. (Ed.). (1973). *Conflict resolution through communication*. New York: Harper & Row.

Johnson, D. W. (1971). Students against the school establishment: Crises intervention in school conflict and organization change. *Journal of School Psychology, 9*, 84–92.

Johnson, D. W., & Lewicki, R. J. (1969). The initiation of superordinate goals. *Journal of Applied Behavioral Science, 5*, 9–24.

Johnson, T. W., & Stinson, J. E. (1975). Role ambiguity, role conflict, and satisfaction: Moderating effects of individual differences. *Journal of Applied Psychology, 60*, 329–333.

Kabanoff, B. (in press). Potential influence structures as sources of interpersonal conflict in groups and organizations. *Organizational Behavior and Human Performance*.

Kahn, R. L., & Boulding, E. (Eds.). (1964). *Power and conflict in organizations*. New York: Basic Books.

Keller, R. T. (1975). Role conflict and ambiguity: Correlates with job satisfaction and values. *Personnel Psychology, 28*, 57–64.

Kelley, J. (1970). Make conflict work for you. *Harvard Business Review, 48*(4), 103–113.

Kelly, J. E., & Nicholson, N. (1980). The causation of strikes: A review of theoretical approaches and the potential contribution of social psychology. *Human Relations, 33*, 853–883.

Kilmann, R. H., & Thomas, K. W. (1978). Four perspectives on conflict management: An attributional framework for organizing descriptive and normative theory. *Academy of Management Review, 3*, 59–68.

Klein, S. M., & Maher, J. R. (1970). Decision-making autonomy and perceived conflict among first-level management. *Personnel Psychology, 23*, 481–492.

Kochan, T. A. (1974). A theory of multilateral collective bargaining in city governments. *Industrial and Labor Relations Review, 27*, 525–542.

Kochan, T. A. (1980). Collective bargaining and organizational behavior research. In B. Straw & L. L. Cummings (Eds.), *Research in organizational behavior* (Vol. 2). Greenwich, CT.: JAI Press.

Kochan, T. A., Huber, G. P., & Cummings, L. L. (1975). Determinants of intra-organizational conflict in collective bargaining in the public sector. *Administrative Science Quarterly, 20*, 10–23.

Kriesberg, L. (1973). *The sociology of social conflicts*. Englewood Cliffs, N.J.: Prentice-Hall.

Krohn, R. G. (1971). Conflict and function: Some basic issues in bureaucratic theory. *British Journal of Sociology, 22*, 115–132.

Labovitz, S., & Miller, J. (1974). Implications of power, conflict, and change in an organizational setting. *Pacific Sociological Review, 17*, 214–239.

Lakin, M. (1972). *Interpersonal encounter: Theory and practice in sensitivity training*. New York: McGraw-Hill.

Lammers, C. J. (1969). Strikes and mutinies: A comparative study of organizational conflicts between rulers and ruled. *Administrative Science Quarterly, 14*, 558–572.

LaTour, S., Houlden, P., Walker, L., & Thibaut, J. (1976). Some determinants of preference for models of conflict resolution. *Journal of Conflict Resolution, 20*, 319–356.

Levi, A. M., & Benjamin, A. (1977). Focus and flexibility in a model of conflict resolution. *Journal of Conflict Resolution, 21*, 405–425.

Levine, S., & White, P. E. (1961). Exchange as a conceptual framework for the study of interorganizational relationships. *Administrative Science Quarterly, 5*, 583–601.

Lindskold, S., & Tedeschi, J. T. (1971). Reward power and attraction in inter-personal conflict. *Psychonomic Science, 22*, 211–213.

Litwak, E. (1961). Models of bureaucracy which permit conflict. *American Journal of Sociology, 67*, 177–184.

London, M., & Howat, G. (1978). The relationship between employee commitment and conflict resolution behavior. *Journal of Vocational Behavior 13*, 1–14.

Lorsch, J. W., & Lawrence, P. R. (Eds.). (1972). *Managing group and intergroup relations*. Homewood, IL.: Irwin-Dorsey.

Louis, M. R. (1977). How individuals conceptualize conflict: Identification of steps in the process and the role of personal/developmental factors. *Human Relations, 30*, 451–467.

Lourenco, S. V., & Glidewell, J. C. (1975). A dialectical analysis of organizational conflict. *Administrative Science Quarterly, 20*, 489–508.

Lundstedt, S. (1970). Conflict management: Preeminent challenge. *Mental Hygiene, 54*, 584–588.

Mack, R. W., & Snyder, R. C. (1957). The analysis of social conflict—Toward an overview and synthesis. *Journal of Conflict Resolution, 1*, 212–248.

Maier, N. R. F. (1970). *Problem-solving and creativity in individuals and groups.* Belmont, CA.: Brooks/Cole.

Mallen, B. (1963). A theory of retailer-supplier conflict, control, and cooperation. *Journal of Retailing, 39*(2), 24–32; 51.

Manning, M. R., Ismail, A. H., & Sherwood, J. J. (1981). Effects of role conflict on selected physiological, affective, and performance variables: A laboratory simulation. *Multivariate Behavioral Research, 16*, 125–141.

Markus, G. B., & Tanter, R. (1972). A conflict model for strategists and managers. *American Behavioral Scientist, 15*, 809–836.

Marsh, J. (1973). Patterns of conflict in American society, 1952–1968. *Sociology and Social Research, 57*, 315–334.

Mason, R. O. (1969). A dialectical approach to strategic planning. *Management Science, 15*, B403–B414.

McKersie, R. B., Perry, C. R., & Walton, R. E. (1965). Intraorganizational bargaining in labor negotiations. *Journal of Conflict Resolution, 9*, 463–481.

McNeil, E. B. (Ed.). (1965). *The nature of human conflict.* Englewood Cliffs, N.J.: Prentice-Hall.

Michener, H. A., Lawler, E. J., & Bacharach, S. B. (1973). Perception of power in conflict situations. *Journal of Personality and Social Psychology, 28*, 155–162.

Miller, G. R. & Simons, H. W. (Eds.). (1974). *Perspectives on communication in social conflict.* Englewood Cliffs, N.J.: Prentice-Hall.

Mortensen C. D. (1974). A transactional paragraph of verbalized social conflict. In G. R. Miller & H. W. Simons (Eds.), *In perspectives on communication in social conflict.* Englewood Cliffs, N.J.: Prentice-Hall.

Mosak, H. H., & LeFevre, C. (1976). The resolution of "intrapersonal conflict." *Journal of Individual Psychology, 32*, 19–26.

Murray, V. V. (1975). Some answered questions on organizational conflict. *Organization and Administrative Sciences, 5*, 35–53.

Neale, M. A., & Bazerman, M. H. (1985). The effects of framing and negotiator overconfidence on bargaining behaviors and outcomes. *Academy of Management Journal, 28*, 34–49.

Neilsen, E. H. (1972). Understanding and managing intergroup conflict. In J. W. Lorsch & P. R. Lawrence (Eds.), *Managing group and intergroup relations.* (pp. 329–343) Homewood, IL.: Irwin-Dorsey.

Nichols, D. R., & Price, K. H. (1976). The auditor-firm conflict: An analysis using concepts of exchange theory. *Accounting Review, 51*, 335–346.

Nutt, P. C. (1979). Calling out and calling off the dogs: Managerial diagnosis in public service organizations. *Academy of Management Review, 4*, 203–214.

Nye, R. D. (1973). *Conflict among humans: Some basic psychological and social-psychological consideration.* New York: Springer.

Oberschall, A. (1978). Theories of social conflict. *Annual Review of Sociology, 4*, 291–315.

Oechsler, W. (1974). Conflict management: The need for a structural approach [Summary]. *Management International Review, 14* (6), 21–23.

Oltman, P. K. Goodenough, D. R., Witkin, H. A., Freedman, N., & Friedman, F. (1975). Psychological differentiation as a factor in conflict resolution. *Journal of Personality and Social Psychology, 32*, 730–736.

Overholt, W. H. (1977). An organizational conflict theory of resolution. *American Behavioral Scientist, 10*, 493–520.

Paltridge, J. G. (1971). Organizational conflict in academia. *California Management Review, 13*(3), 85–94.

Paul, R. J., & Schooler, R. D. (1970). An analysis of performance standards and generation conflict in academia. *Academy of Management Journal, 13*, 212–216.

Perry, J. L., & Levine, C. H. (1976). An interorganizational analysis of power, conflict, and settlements in public sector collective bargaining. *American Political Science Review, 70*, 1185–1201.

Peterson, R. B., & Tracy, L. N. (1976). A behavioral model of problem solving in labor negotiations. *British Journal of Industrial Relations, 14*, 159–173.

Pondy, L. R. (1966). A systems theory of organizational conflict. *Academy of Management Journal, 9*, 246–256.

Prein, H. (1984). A contingency approach for conflict intervention. *Group and Organization Studies, 9*, 81–102.

Pruitt, D. G. (1983). Strategic choice in negotiation. *American Behavioral Scientist, 27*, 167–194.

Pruitt, D. G. (1983). Achieving integrative agreements. In M. H. Bazerman & R. J. Lewicki (Eds.), *Negotiations in Organizations* (pp. 35–50). Beverly Hills, CA.: Sage.

Putnam, L. L., & Jones, T. S. (1982). Reciprocity in negotiations: An analysis of bargaining interaction. *Communication Monographs, 49*, 171–191.

Rapoport, A., & Chammah, A. M. (1965). *Prisoner's dilemma: A study in conflict and cooperation.* Ann Arbor: University of Michigan Press.

Rappoport, L. H. (1965). Interpersonal conflict in cooperative and uncertain situations. *Journal of Experimental Social Psychology, 1*, 323–333.

Rico, L. (1964). Organizational conflict: A framework for reappraisal. *Industrial Management Review, 6*(1), 67–79.

Roark, A. E. (1978). Interpersonal conflict management. *Personnel and Guidance Journal, 56*, 400–402.

Roark, A., & Wilkinson, L. (1979). Approaches to conflict management. *Group and Organization Studies, 4*, 440–452.

Robert, M. (1982). *Managing conflict: From the inside out.* Austin, TX.: Learning Concepts.

Rose, G. L., Menasco, M. B., & Curry, D. J. (1982). When disagreement facilitates performance in judgement tasks: Effects of different forms of cognitive conflict, information environments, and human information processing characteristics. *Organizational Behavior and Human Performance, 29*, 287–306.

Rosenbloom, B. (1973). Conflict and channel efficiency: Some conceptual models for the decision maker. *Journal of Marketing, 37*(3), 26–30.

Rosenhan, D. L. (1973). On being sane in insane places. *Science, 179*, 250–258.

Salipante, P. F., & Aram, J. D. (1984). The role of organizational procedures in the resolution of social conflict. *Human Organization, 43*, 9–15.

Sayeed, O. B., & Mathur, H. B. (1980). Leadership behavior and conflict management strategies. *Vikalpa, 5*, 275–282.

Schellenberg, J. A. (1982). *The science of conflict.* New York: Oxford University Press.

Schuler, R. S., Aldag, R. J., & Brief, A. P. (1977). Role conflict and ambiguity: A scale analysis. *Organizational Behavior and Human Performance, 20,* 111–128.

Schutz, W. C. (1958). Interpersonal underworld. *Harvard Business Review, 36*(4), 123–135.

Schwenk, C. R. (1984). Devil's advocacy in managerial decision-making. *Journal of Management Studies, 21*(2), 153–168.

Scott, W. G. (1965). *The management of conflict: Appeals systems in organizations.* Homewood, IL.: Irwin-Dorsey.

Seidl, F. W. (1977). Conflict and conflict resolution in residential treatment. *Child Care Quarterly, 6,* 267–278.

Sell, M. V., Brief, A. P., & Schuler, R. S. (1981). Role conflict and role ambiguity: Integration of the literature and directions for further research, *Human Relations, 34,* 43–71.

Shamir, B. (1980). Between service and servility: Role conflict in subordinate service roles. *Human Relations, 33,* 741–756.

Shea, G. P. (1980). The study of bargaining and conflict behavior: Broadening the conceptual area. *Journal of Conflict Resolution, 24,* 706–741.

Sheane, D. (1980). When and how to intervene in conflict. *Personnel Journal, 59,* 515–518.

Shockley-Zalabak, P. (1981). The effects of sex differences on the preference for utilization of conflict styles of managers in a work setting: An exploratory study. *Public Personnel Management Journal, 10,* 289–295.

Shuptrine, F. K., & Foster, J. R. (1976). Monitoring channel conflict with evaluations from the retail level. *Journal of Retailing, 52*(1), 55–74.

Simmons, R. G. (1968). The role conflict of the first-line supervisor: An experimental study. *American Journal of Sociology, 73,* 482–495.

Simon, H. A. (1972). Persuasion in social conflicts: A critique of prevailing conceptions and a framework for future research. *Speech Monographs, 39,* 227–247.

Slack, B. D., & Cook, J. O. (1973). Authoritarian behavior in a conflict situation. *Journal of Personality and Social Psychology, 25,* 130–136.

Smith, C. G. (Ed.). (1971). *Conflict resolution: Contributions of the behavioral sciences.* South Bend: Notre Dame University Press.

Smith, K. K. (1975). The values and dangers of power conflict. *Contemporary Australian Management, 3,* 9–23.

Smith, K. K. (1982). *Groups in conflict: Prisons in disguise.* Dubuque, IA.: Kendall/Hunt.

Snyder, D. (1975). Institutional setting and industrial conflict: Comparative analysis of France, Italy and the United States. *American Sociological Review, 40,* 259–278.

Sorensen, J. E., & Sorensen, R. L. (1974). The conflict of professionals in bureaucratic organizations. *Administrative Science Quarterly, 19,* 98–106.

Spiegal, J. P. (1969). Campus conflict and professional egos. *Transaction, 6,* 41–50.

Stagner, R. (1956). *Psychology of industrial conflict*. New York: John Wiley.

Stanley, J. D. (1981). Dissent in organizations. *Academy of Management Review, 6*, 13–19.

Stavig, G. R., & Barnett, L. D. (1977). Group size and societal conflict, *Human Relations, 30*, 761–765.

Stephenson, T. E. (1960). The causes of management conflict. *California Management Conflict, 11*(2), 90–97.

Stern, L. W. (1971). Antitrust implications of a sociological interpretation of competition, conflict, and cooperation in the marketplace. *Antitrust Bulletin, 16*, 509–530.

Stern, L. W., Schulz, R. A., Jr., & Grabner, J. R., Jr. (1973). The power base-conflict relationship: Preliminary findings. *Social Science Quarterly, 54*, 412–419.

Stern, L. W., Sternthal, B., & Craig, C. S. (1973). A parasimulation of inter-organizational conflict. *International Journal of Group Tensions, 3*, 68–90.

Stern, L. W., Sternthal, B., & Craig, C. S. (1975). Strategies for managing inter-organizational conflict: A laboratory paradigm. *Journal of Applied Psychology, 60*, 472–482.

Stewart, K. L. (1978). What a university ombudsman does: A sociological study of everybody conduct. *Journal of Higher Education, 49*, 1–22.

Strauss, G. (1964). Work-flow frictions, interfunctional rivalry, and professionalism: A case study of purchasing agents. *Human Organization, 23*, 137–149.

Stymne, B. (1968). Interdepartmental communication and intraorganizational strain. *Acta Sociologica, 11*, 82–100.

Teaching how to cope with workplace conflicts (1980, February 18). *Business Week*, pp. 136, 139.

Thamhain, H. J., & Wilemon, D. L. (1975). Conflict management in project life cycles. *Sloan Management Review, 16*(3), 31–50.

Thamhain, H. J., & Wilemon, D. L. (1977). Leadership, conflict, and program management effectiveness. *Sloan Management Review, 19*(1), 69–89.

Thomas, J. W. & Bennis, W. G. (Eds.). (1972). *The management of change and conflict*. Middlesex, England: Penguin Books.

Thomas, K. W. (1978). Introduction: Conflict and the collaborative ethic. *California Management Review, 21*(2) 56–60.

Thomas, K. W., Jamieson, D. W., & Moore, R. K. (1978). Conflict and collaboration: Some concluding observations. *California Management Review, 21*(2), 91–95.

Thomas, K. W., & Kilmann, R. H. (1975). The social desirability variable in organizational research: An alternative explanation for reported findings. *Academy of Management Journal, 18*, 741–752.

Thomas, K. W., & Pondy, L. P. (1977). Toward an "intent" model of conflict management among principal parties. *Human Relations, 30*, 1089–1102.

Thompson, J. D. (1960). Organizational management of conflict. *Administrative Science Quarterly, 4*, 489–509.

Thompson, V. A. (1961). Hierarchy, specialization, and organizational conflict. *Administrative Science Quarterly, 5*, 485–551.

Tjosvold, D., & Johnson, D. W. (1977). Effects of controversy on cognitive perspective taking. *Journal of Educational Psychology, 69*, 679–685.

Tjosvold, D., & Deemer, D. K. (1980). Effects of controversy within a cooperative or competitive context on organizational decision making. *Journal of Applied Psychology, 65*, 590–595.

Todd, F.J., Hammond, K. R., & Wilkins, M. M. (1966). Differential effects of ambiguous and exact feedback on two-person conflict and compromise. *Journal of Conflict Resolution, 10*, 88–97.

Turner, J. H. (1975). A strategy for reformulating the dialectical and functional theories of conflict. *Social Forces, 53*, 433–444.

Turner, J. H. (1975). Marx and Simmel revisited: Reassessing the foundations of conflict theory. *Social Forces, 53*, 618–627.

Twomey, D. F. (1978). The effects of power properties on conflict resolution. *Academy of Management Review, 1*, 144–150.

Vliert, E. van de (1981). Siding and other reactions to a conflict: A theory of escalation toward outsiders. *Journal of Conflict Resolution, 25*, 495–520.

Vliert, E. van de (1985). Escalative intervention in small group conflicts. *Journal of Applied Behavioral Science, 39*, 32–39.

Walker, O. D., Churchill, G. A., & Ford, N. M. (1975). Organizational determinants of the industrial salesman's role conflict and ambiguity. *Journal of Marketing, 39*, 32–39.

Wall, J. A., Jr. (1985). *Negotiation: Theory and practice.* Glenview, IL.: Scott, Foresman.

Wall, J. A., Jr., & Adams, J. S. (1974). Some variables affecting a constituent's evaluations of and behavior toward a boundary role occupant. *Organizational Behavior and Human Performance, 11*, 390–408.

Walton, R. E. (1967). Third party roles in interdepartmental conflict. *Industrial Relations, 7*, 29–43.

Walton, R. E. (1969). *Interpersonal peacemaking: Confrontations and third party consultation.* Reading, MA.: Addison-Wesley.

Walton, R. E. (1970). A problem-solving workshop on border conflicts in Eastern Africa. *Journal of Applied Behavioral Science, 6*, 453–489.

Walton, R. E., Dutton, J. M., & Cafferty, T. P. (1969). Organizational context and interdepartmental conflict. *Administrative Science Quarterly, 14*, 522–542.

Walton, R. E., & McKersie, R. B. (1966). Behavioral dilemmas in mixed-motive decision making. *Behavioral Science, 2*, 370–384.

Wedge, B. (1971). A psychiatric model for intercession in intergroup conflict. *Journal of Applied Behavioral Science, 7*, 733–761.

Welds, K. (1979). Conflict in the work place and how to manage it. *Personnel Journal, 58*, 380–383.

Whetten, D. A. (1978). Coping with incompatible expectations: An integrated view of role conflict. *Administrative Science Quarterly, 23*, 254–271.

Zald, M. N. (1962). Power balance and staff conflict in correctional institutions. *Administrative Science Quarterly, 7*, 22–49.

Zaleznik, A (1967). Management of disappointment. *Harvard Business Review, 45* (6), 59–70.

Zand, D. E. (1972). Trust and managerial problem solving. *Administrative Science Quarterly, 17*, 229–239.

Zacker, J., & Bard, M. (1973). Effects of conflict management training on police performance. *Journal of Applied Psychology, 58*, 202–208.

Ziller, R. C., Zeigler, H., Gregor, G. L., Styskal, R. A., & Peak, W. (1969). The neutral in a communication network under conditions of conflict. *American Behavioral Scientist, 13*, 265–282.

Author Index

Subject Index

ABOUT THE AUTHOR

M. AFZALUR RAHIM is Professor of Management at Western Kentucky University, Bowling Green, Kentucky. Until 1982 he was Professor of Management at Youngstown State University, Ohio.

Dr. Rahim has published widely in the areas of organizational behavior and management. His articles have appeared in *Academy of Management Journal, Human Relations, Management International Review, Personnel Journal, Journal of Social Psychology, Psychological Reports, Perceptual and Motor Skills, Journal of Psychology, and Journal of General Psychology.* His recent publications include *Rahim Organizational Conflict Inventory-I and II* and their *Manual* (Consulting Psychologists Press, 1983).

Dr. Rahim holds B. Com. Honours and M. Com. degrees from Dacca University (Bangladesh), and M.B.A. and Ph.D. degrees from Miami University (Ohio) and University of Pittsburgh (Pennsylvania), respectively. He teaches courses on strategic management, behavioral science, and research methodology.